GOLD
PANNING
IN BRITISH COLUMBIA

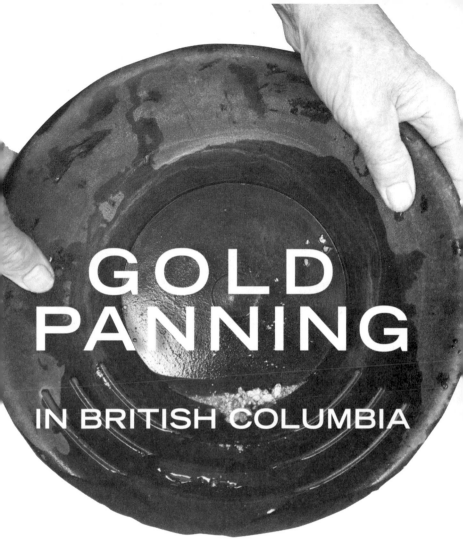

GOLD PANNING

IN BRITISH COLUMBIA

JIM LEWIS AND SUSAN CAMPANY

H
HERITAGE

VICTORIA · VANCOUVER · CALGARY

Heritage House Publishing Company Ltd.
heritagehouse.ca

LIBRARY AND ARCHIVES CANADA CATALOGUING IN PUBLICATION

Lewis, Jim, 1939–
    Gold panning in British Columbia / Jim Lewis and Susan Campany.

Includes index.
Issued also in electronic formats.
ISBN 978-1-927527-12-2

    1. Prospecting—British Columbia—Guidebooks. 2. British Columbia—Gold discoveries—Guidebooks. 3. British Columbia—Guidebooks. I. Campany, Susan II. Title.

FC3820.G6L48 2013   622'.184109711   C2012-907043-2

Edited by Lara Kordic
Proofread by Kate Scallion
Cover and book design by Jacqui Thomas
Cover photos by BanksPhotos/iStockphoto.com (gold pan), kickers/iStockphoto.com (nuggets)
All interior photos, unless otherwise credited, are reproduced with permission from the British Columbia Ministry of Energy and Mines.

 The interior of this book was produced on 30% post-consumer recycled paper, processed chlorine free and printed with vegetable-based inks.

Heritage House acknowledges the financial support for its publishing program from the Government of Canada through the Canada Book Fund (CBF), Canada Council for the Arts and the province of British Columbia through the British Columbia Arts Council and the Book Publishing Tax Credit.

   Canadian   Patrimoine
Heritage   canadien

17 16 15 14 13 1 2 3 4 5

Printed in Canada

CONTENTS

ACKNOWLEDGEMENTS

It is with a great deal of sorrow that I mention the passing of my wife, Susan, on March 29, 2013, after a battle with cancer. She was an excellent and enthusiastic gold-panning partner and prospecting companion, as well as a wonderful wife and co-author. She was very outgoing and made many friends in all the areas we visited, and she will be sadly missed.

I would also like to acknowledge Klaus Maak, an excellent prospector and friend to both Susan and me.

— Jim Lewis

BEFORE YOU START

. . . .

If you have read our previous books, you will be familiar with the "Essentials" section which contains instructions on how to pan for gold and stake claims. Even if you are an experienced gold panner, we urge you to review this section as it contains some new information, including changes to provincial regulations.

If you are new to the Creeks of Gold series, welcome! This volume combines all the material from our previous three books—covering the Cariboo region; the Fraser, Thompson and Columbia River Systems; and Southwestern BC and Vancouver Island—as well as a new section on the Okanagan and the Kootenays. We have selected a wide range of panning gems scattered throughout the province based on our own extensive experience prospecting in the field, and we have included the mining history of each area, including interesting facts obtained from the BC Ministry of Mines annual reports dating back over a century. We have personally panned each and every creek mentioned in this book. Because this book is geared toward recreational panners, we have focused on golden opportunities that are relatively easy to access; however, some of the areas discussed in the book are a little harder to get to. Accessibility of each location is indicated by the following symbols:

✳ = ready access

✳✳ = access is more difficult

✳✳✳ = very little or no road access (for experienced hikers only)

For ease of reading, two conventions have been used throughout:

- All distances are estimates.
- Directions assume you are facing upstream.

The maps are designed to provide a reference for specific creek locations. **Due to size limitations, however, it was impossible to include all the creeks mentioned in the book on these maps.** We recommend that you acquire more detailed maps when visiting specific sites.

Good luck wherever these leads take you, and remember to have fun!

THE ESSENTIALS

. . . .

Nothing lights up the human imagination quite like the flash of gold. For many of us, the great stories of bonanza strikes and glorious riches have become like fairy tales—pleasant illusions of glittering creeks of yesteryear. But a deeper look, both in the ground and in the mining records of British Columbia, reveals that untold facets of discovery still await the curious wanderer. In fact, the province's early gold seekers, who had to wager everything on a chance at fulfilling their dreams, weren't anywhere near as fortunate as today's recreational prospectors, who are free to meander through BC's splendid valleys and dabble away in the gold creeks with nothing more sophisticated than a round plastic pan.

The brilliant metal was first mined in BC in the late 1850s, when the province was a new English colony. Tens of thousands of fortune hunters made their way north from California, following the mighty Fraser River to the goldfields. When the Cariboo gold rush began to decline in the late 1880s, gold was still selling for $16 an ounce. Its value was fixed at various levels until 1971, when the international price was allowed to float according to demand.

With prices reaching record highs in recent years ($1,400 per ounce at the time of printing), it's easy to see why gold has retained its lustre and why it continues to lure prospectors to remote and uncharted places. We'll let these adventurers pursue their more distant dreams, however, for theirs is not the road travelled in this guide.

Rather, *Gold Panning in British Columbia* points toward accessible sites, documented finds, pleasant experiences and the ultimate thrill of discovering gold. Hikers, campers, families—anyone who samples the creeks in this guide—will quickly see proof that the best places to search are the very areas that produced gold in the past. Here your chances for success are far greater than wandering about in virgin areas with no history of discovery. For despite all the gold recovered in BC over the years, there is plenty still waiting to be found.

With recreational panning you never lose. No matter what unfolds—be it a day of exciting discovery or one of peaceful exploration—the experience is a treasure. Assuming you are here more for excitement than peace, the rest of this chapter covers what you need to know.

1 WHERE TO SEARCH

Every year spring torrents scrape more gold from mineral veins in the high country, carrying flakes and nuggets downstream. Because it is so dense, gold sinks to the streambed in predictable locations. Easily distinguished from other minerals by its weight and brilliant colour, gold gradually works its way through surface gravels and settles on bedrock. One of the most critical aspects of prospecting is developing an eye for the places where gold tends to accumulate.

Surveying a Creek

The most basic rule of finding gold is to look for areas where natural obstructions slow the current, allowing heavier material to sink to the bottom. The swifter the flow, the less likely that there will be gold deposits. The best areas are easiest to spot during spring runoff or after heavy rainfall. On straight-flowing creeks, look for large rocks, sand and gravel bars or uprooted trees—anything that interrupts the water's flow. Iron often originates from the same mineral veins as gold, and since it is almost as heavy as gold, it tends to accumulate in similar places. Iron pyrites and black sand (concentrated iron) are gold indicators. **Any black sand you find should be panned.** Iron pyrites? Well, they're the infamous fool's gold. Fortunately they can be distinguished from the real McCoy by their sharp edges and brittle texture. Iron pyrites shatter if you apply pressure to them with a knife blade. Gold is much softer and will become rounded after travelling a short distance downstream. If you do happen to stumble upon rough nuggets, catch your breath and take a good look around. Assuming they haven't tumbled from someone else's poke, chances are you've struck pay dirt close to the source!

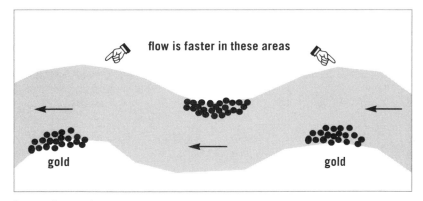

Survey the creek.

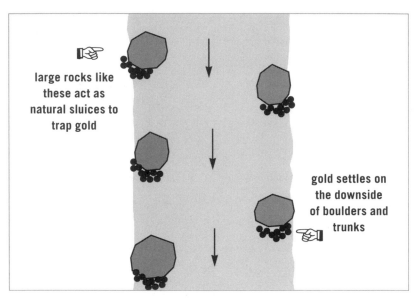

large rocks like these act as natural sluices to trap gold

gold settles on the downside of boulders and trunks

Watch for obstructions in the flow.

SEARCH TIPS

1 Gold is heavier than sand and gravel: it works its way to bedrock.

2 Focus on areas where creeks slow down.

3 Explore the streambed behind large rocks. Gold accumulates on the downstream side.

4 Check under uprooted trees; the creek bed may be exposed.

5 Watch for iron pyrites and black sand.

Locations

British Columbia's rich gold history includes spectacular discoveries in many areas of the province—Atlin, Boundary and Big Bend, Cassiar, the East and West Kootenays, the Fraser River and its tributaries, the

Similkameen, the Thompson River and its tributaries, the Okanagan, Omenica, Vancouver Island, Haida Gwaii and the McLeod River north of Prince George. The heaviest concentrations have been found in the Cariboo region: Barkerville, Quesnel Forks, Likely, Horsefly, Quesnel Lake, the Quesnel River area and the Fraser River.

A geological band of gold runs from Alaska and Yukon Territory right through the heart of British Columbia. These extensive deposits, distributed mainly by the action of glaciers and erosion, continue to shift and evolve through natural forces. Glacial action during the retreat of the last ice age, some 15,000 years ago, sprinkled new deposits of gold all along BC's creeks and rivers. Scraping the mountain peaks and carving out valleys, huge blankets of flowing ice ground everything in their path and cast off gold and other minerals in their wake.

Bear in mind that the flow of creeks is ever changing. Earth tremors, landslides and other natural forces can dramatically alter a creek's course, leaving a dry channel where mineral-laden water used to flow. Understanding these ancient channels, also called glacial channels and pre-glacial channels, is an important part of the prospecting mystique. Just remember that **old channels don't always follow the course of an existing stream, but they are often rich sources of gold.** In many cases, these channels have never been mined.

When panning, always be alert for changes in gold content from one spot to the next. If a promising area suddenly turns barren, it's likely an old channel traverses the creek and you've passed beyond it, losing the gold's trail. Go back and carefully rework the area. Check the banks above the water line. Old channels are often wide and, like surface creeks and streams, tend to meander along crooks and bends. As a general rule, **glacial channels are richer and tend to run in a northwest and southeast direction**, with smaller streams flowing in from the sides.

A visual survey of creek banks is easy to do and may reveal the path of older channels. Climb up to level land, lie flat on your stomach and look for even the slightest hump or depression in the ground. Scan the terrain from both sides of the creek. If there are any irregularities, sample the banks on both sides of the creek at that location, above the high-water mark. Although primitive, this approach is as effective today as it was when prospectors were first exploring BC's creeks.

Since erosion continues to deposit gold in new locations, panning expeditions can be especially rewarding after a hard winter. When snow and ice melt, huge volumes of water rush down from the headwaters. This annual runoff rakes away boulders, trees, gravel and topsoil, grinding creek banks and scouring streambeds. Along with the flood, gold is swept farther downstream—sometimes settling many miles from its original source.

Gold is unlikely to settle in a section of creek that flows over exposed bedrock. **Always check gravel banks**, though, at creek level and higher up, as well as any cracks and crevices in the rock. The search tips described earlier will help you locate the best prospects. If you can, go to high ground and try to visualize the creek's flow during high runoff.

2 METHODS OF RECOVERY

Patience is possibly the single most important trait necessary for good prospecting. Recovering gold is a methodical process and should not be rushed.

The Gold Pan

For those travelling light, this is the only way to go. The most popular model is the plastic pan with built-in riffles, little ridges that help trap the gold. These pans have replaced the traditional metal pan. They are resistant to light and acid, do not corrode and are strong enough to withstand rough treatment. Green is the best colour—it clearly displays black sand and is ideal for spotting fine gold. Pans range in size from 15 to 45 centimetres (6 to 18 inches) in diameter, the most common being the 30- to 35-centimetre (12- to 14-inch) models. These are easy to handle and cost less than $20.

Panning Technique

Always work your way upstream to avoid disturbing unpanned waters. Sample the creek every 6 to 9 metres (20 or 30 feet), watching for any sudden changes that might announce the presence of an old channel. Fill the pan with creek-bed gravel to the top riffle, or two-thirds full. Submerge the pan, mix and knead its contents with your hands, breaking lumps of clay or soil to free any gold trapped inside. Continue mixing in water, and some of the finest material will wash away. Pick out the surface rocks and pebbles and discard them.

Now you're ready to begin in earnest. Keeping the riffled portion away from you, resubmerge the pan and raise the rim to just below the water's surface. Tilt the pan slightly away so the nearside rim is just above water level. Shake the pan from side to side with a light circular motion. This technique keeps the lighter material in suspension and works it out of the pan,

Good technique involves tilting the pan and swirling it to concentrate the heaviest materials on the bottom.

leaving gold and other heavy materials around the pan's bottom edges.

Every now and then, lift the pan clear of the creek and shake it vigorously, using the same circular motion to concentrate the gold and heavy sands. With your thumb, again scrape away pebbles and fine materials that rise to the top. Continue panning until only the heaviest material remains. The whole operation should take about 5 or 10 minutes (you'll get faster with experience). Be careful to ensure that no gold washes away in the final stages. If you have a tub or pail handy, use it instead of the stream to finish panning.

Coarse gold can now be removed with tweezers. Since gold does not respond to magnetism, a magnet is ideal for extracting any black sand or iron pyrites. The remaining material should be dried. The finest gold can be recovered by carefully blowing the dried sand away or by using mercury.

1920s prospectors work the Cariboo River with metal pans.

The Last Step

Purifying the gold residue takes some ingenuity. Here are two simple techniques that have emerged over the years.

A) Mercury and a Chamois Cloth

Placed in a gold pan along with the sand tailings, mercury will amalgamate fine gold, absorbing the tiny particles into a ball. The gold can then be extracted by squeezing the mercury through a chamois cloth.

B) Mercury and a Baked Potato

Alternatively, the trusty potato can be pressed into service. Cut a large potato in two and hollow out one half for the amalgam. Rejoin the halves and cover the whole potato with aluminum foil. After baking it thoroughly, remove the foil and squeeze the potato to drain the mercury. (Although it may be tempting, don't eat the potato!)

The remaining gold can be further purified by placing it in a metal bowl and applying heat, or by using a retort, a vessel in which substances such as mercury are distilled by heat.

ABOUT MERCURY

Mercury is a rather noxious substance that needs to be handled with care. Fortunately, only a small quantity (30 to 60 grams, or one or two ounces) is needed to amalgamate fine gold. These days, it's not that easy to find: mining or laboratory suppliers are your best bets.

Prospecting High Banks

Gold will be deposited high up on creek banks during spring runoff. In dry season these areas may be well above the waterline and hard to reach. Here's a simple method for prospecting a high bank when you plan to return some time later.

Look for a small, dry ravine—one that sees water only during high runoff. Clean out the lower section of this gully, removing rocks, brush and limbs. Lay a sheet of plastic, five to six metres (15 to 20 feet) wide, about 15 metres (50 feet) up the ravine from the main stream. Dig the sheet in at the top to hold it in place, then secure it with rocks along the top and sides. Lay a series of bigger rocks at the bottom to trap material that washes down.

The following spring, or after heavy runoff, pan the material that has collected. This "float" may contain quartz bearing gold or other signs that the higher banks would be worth closer inspection. (When you're done, be sure to pack the plastic out with you.)

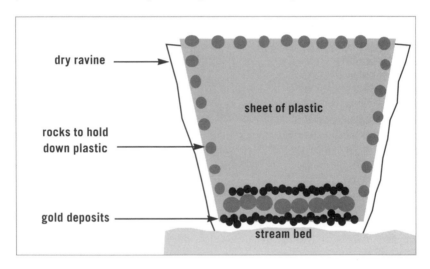

Other Methods

If you do not obtain a Free Miner Certificate (FMC), prospecting tools for recreational panning are restricted to the gold pan and shovel. Other tools—such as the dredges, sluice boxes and rockers—undoubtedly process gravel more quickly than a pan and may be bought or built with portability in mind. However, using them involves more regulations.

3 REGULATIONS AND SAFETY

Like fishing, hunting, driving and nearly everything else, prospecting comes with rules and regulations. Given that claim jumping might be the West's second-oldest profession (after prostitution), these regulations are there for a reason. Moreover, the very nature of wandering around on unfamiliar ground means that common safety rules and respect for wildlife are relevant to the gold seeker's experience. Much of the information that facilitates a gold panning expedition comes from the Mineral Titles website (www.mtonline.gov.bc.ca), as well as the Mineral Tenure Act (www.bclaws.ca/EPLibraries/bclaws_new/ document/ID/freeside/00_96292_01), which outlines the duties and responsibilities of free miners and administrators. Updates to the act and regulations are periodically posted online, so always consult the website before you head out.

Even if you are only panning recreationally, we strongly recommend that you purchase a Free Miner Certificate. Just as a fishing licence allows you to bait a hook, this certificate is required to stake a claim or use more sophisticated tools. At the time of printing, it costs $25 per annum for those aged 18 to 64 to obtain an FMC, and the certificate is free of charge for those over 65. No matter your age, you must renew your FMC every year.

Trespassing on someone else's claim carries strict penalties, so always check the Mineral Titles website, under the subheading "Search for Mineral/Placer/Coal Titles," before setting out. Following set procedures, making sure all the paperwork is done and paying the appropriate fee are all vital steps in securing a valid claim. Do your research and you should have no trouble.

For the more dedicated prospector, staking a placer is an exciting step. It grants you the exclusive rights to surface minerals on a section of Crown land. Research and timing are essential ingredients for success, and the regulations are relatively straightforward. Tutorials and information can be obtained at www.MTOnline.gov.bc.ca.

MAINTAINING CLAIMS

No placer claim lasts forever. This is good news for the recreational panner, as previously staked areas are constantly coming open again. Like other forms of ownership, a claim for surface mineral rights invokes certain responsibilities. The law sets out minimum annual requirements, which must be met to maintain a valid claim. Otherwise, the claim is cancelled. It's as simple as that.

The annual requirements can be met in one of two ways:

1 Complete and record the necessary exploration and development work, or

2 Pay a fee in lieu of this work. Mining records are reviewed regularly, and neglected claims are cancelled on their anniversary date. Once claims are cancelled, anyone is eligible to restake and register them.

Buy the relevant topographic map for your area of interest. These maps detail roads, rivers, creeks, elevations and land contours and will help keep you on track. BC topographic maps are inexpensive and not too difficult to find, but you may have to go to a specialty map shop. Some bookstores also supply them.

It's worth noting that although placer claims come in various shapes and sizes, a full-size claim measures 1,000 by 500 metres (3,000 by 1,600 feet) and is rectangular. Contrary to what you might expect, a placer claim is staked with only two posts. The area is marked by running a straight line along the length of the claim from an initial post to a final post. This line, called a location line, bisects the claim.

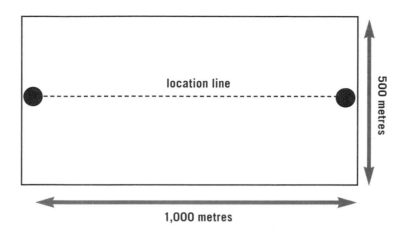

location line

500 metres

1,000 metres

A full-size claim.

Other people's gold claims aren't the only property rights you'll encounter along the trail. Follow directions or seek permission when using logging or mining roads, ranchers' tracks or other private rights of way. When travelling in the backcountry, respect the environment. Close gates behind you and ensure that fences and cattleguards are secure.

Although bear or cougar attacks are relatively rare, stay alert. Most mishaps occur when people surprise an animal, so make plenty of noise. **Constant vigilance is essential if you are prospecting in grizzly country.**

Before setting off, let someone know where you are headed. If you don't know anyone in the area, notify the RCMP, the local fire department or the district forestry office and always report back to your contact when your prospecting trip is done. Unless you are an experienced outdoors person, travelling alone isn't a good idea. If you are heading off to explore, carry a map of the area where you are planning to explore and tell someone where you are going and when you expect to be back. Carry a GPS and/or a compass and mark your trail with flagging tape. Stick to your original planned destination and don't deviate.

A backcountry rescue can be costly and time consuming. If you do become lost or disoriented, though, it's best to stay in one place and wait to be found. Don't try to hike out, especially after dark. Light a fire, if it's permitted. Do what you can to keep warm and dry.

4 EQUIPMENT

When setting out on a prospecting adventure you should consult two separate checklists. The first one covers the basics—a list of musts for prospecting in the wilderness. The second list deals with optional equipment that will improve your chances of success.

The Basics

Clothing Loose-fitting clothes, raingear and sturdy footwear are the hiker's second skin. Pack along extra socks, too; your feet will likely get soaked.

Compass It is essential to set the declination before striking out. Nearby metal (such as a belt buckle, pocket change or a vehicle) can affect compass readings, so move away from any potentially magnetic source when you fix the compass setting.

Gold Pan A variety of sizes can be purchased or ordered through most hardware stores.

First Aid Kit Include Band-Aids, gauze, bandages and disinfectant. Depending on the season, consider adding insect repellant and bear spray.

Knife A sturdy folding or hunting knife is best.

Matches Pack a generous supply in a waterproof container.

Shovel A long-handled shovel is essential for digging gravel and sampling material below the surface.

Small Vial A film canister or pill bottle is ideal for storing recovered gold. Fill the vial with water to prevent loss of fine gold in windy conditions.

Optional Prospecting Gear

Altimeter Available in both metric and imperial scales, an altimeter shows your elevation. To be accurate, the instrument must be set at a known point above sea level. An altimeter is affected by barometric conditions, so it has to be reset daily. Topographic maps have contours to show elevation—at known locations you can reset your altimeter to these.

Hammer Carried on your belt, a geologist's hammer (hammer face on one end, pick on the other) is great for working creek banks and breaking rocks.

Magnifying Glass A 10-power glass will help spot fragments of gold. A folding pocket model is ideal.

Magnet and Tweezers A magnet will remove black sand from gold concentrate; wrap it in plastic for easy cleaning. Tweezers handle coarse gold that's too small to be grasped with fingers.

Plastic Sheet A large plastic sheet can be useful for prospecting high banks and will double as a rain cover or tarp.

Pry Bar A small pry bar or chisel will widen crevices and cracks in bedrock. The chisel can be worked into deeper areas to recover trapped gold.

Suction Gun and Brushes A syringe-type suction gun with a long tube can be used to draw material out of hard-to-reach places. For wider cracks, a small brush with stiff bristles can be also used. Some prospectors pack along narrow paint brushes for this purpose. A kitchen knife or steel spoon will also prove handy.

5 PROSPECTING TALK—LEARNING THE LINGO

Like any field, prospecting has its own special terms. You'll encounter some of these throughout the book.

Auriferous Gold bearing.

Bar A raised area located above normal water level in the river. During spring runoff it can be temporarily covered. Each year more gold is deposited in these sand or gravel areas. There have been some spectacular gold discoveries in river bars.

Bedrock The rock bottom of a stream or river.

Benches Areas of flat or slightly inclined ground lying immediately above creeks and rivers. The banks can yield excellent returns.

Black Sand Iron concentrate, usually composed of hemetite or magnetite.

Coarse Gold and Fine Gold Nuggets, usually discovered close to their original source. Fine gold has usually travelled a greater distance than coarse gold and is more rounded and flattened by the action of water.

Crevice or Crack A fissure in rock where gold can be trapped and accumulate.

False Bedrock An area of heavy clay or cemented gravel overlying real bedrock.

Fineness A term to determine the purity of gold. Gold's fineness in most streams ranges from percentages in the low 700s to the mid-900s, with 1,000 percent being the finest.

Float The material washed down from high banks during runoff.

Fool's Gold Minerals that are often mistaken for gold, such as iron pyrites or mica.

Fraction A mining claim that's less than full size. A fraction usually occurs when an area is staked between two or more existing claims.

Gradient The descending slope of a river or creek, denoting its elevation.

Grizzly A heavy screen placed on top of a framework to prevent rocks from entering sluice boxes. (If someone yells "grizzly" and hightails it, though, it might mean something else!)

Hydraulic Mining Water forced under high pressure to wash hillsides and creek banks into sluice boxes. This method of mining is no longer allowed.

Lode or Lode Vein Gold veins in solid rock, the source of most placer gold found in streams.

Moss Another potential source of trapped gold; break it up and pan it.

Nugget A lump of solid gold that can be minuscule or weigh many ounces.

Oil Fish oils sometimes coat gold, especially in large spawning rivers such as the Fraser. Gold coated in oil sometimes floats.

Overburden The non-gold-bearing gravel, rocks and clay that is overlying gold and settled closer to bedrock.

Quartz Most gold deposits are veins found in quartz, which can be colourless, white, rose-coloured, brown-stained or green. Also called wire gold.

Rocker Box A sieve mounted on a sloping rocker base that has riffles or canvas collection blankets to trap gold.

Sluice Box An open-ended trough with riffles on the floor, positioned in the creek so that water washes over the river gravels shovelled into the box.

Sniping Cleaning old mine dumps and tailings, as well as cracks and crevices in bedrock.

Tailings Dumps, mounds and ponds at old mine sites. Tailings have been known to produce nuggets of considerable size.

Troy Weight Also known as apothecary weight, this system, commonly used by assayers, is based on the pound containing 5,760 grains, or 340 grams (12 ounces) of 480 grains each. By contrast, the more commonly used avoirdupois or US customary system of weight is based on 7,000 grains, or 453 grams (16 ounces) of 437.5 grains each.

In troy weight, the system used for precious metals and gems,

24 grains = one pennyweight

20 pennyweights = one troy ounce

12 troy ounces = one troy pound

1 troy pound = 0.8232 US customary pounds, or 373.24 grams.

Value An estimate of gold's worth as compared with the effort required to recover it.

Wing Dam A method used to divert a short section of the creek into another area so that the gold can be mined from the exposed underlying bedrock.

PART
I

THE CARIBOO

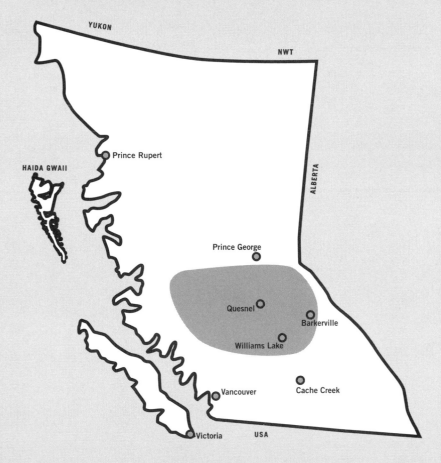

YUKON

NWT

Prince Rupert

HAIDA GWAII

ALBERTA

Prince George

Quesnel

Barkerville

Williams Lake

Vancouver

Cache Creek

Victoria

USA

THE CARIBOO'S GOLD-BEARING CREEKS

The gold history of the Cariboo is legendary and has been well documented. Over the years, many thousands have prospected and mined the slopes and valleys of this rich country. In spite of all the attention, though, the gold-bearing creeks of the Cariboo have never been worked to their full potential.

Until relatively recent times, it wasn't easy to track the Cariboo's gold secrets; the lack of roads and easy transportation made the region inaccessible to all but the most determined and hardy prospectors travelling on foot. These adventurers courted fortune with little more than the shirts on their backs and the most basic of tools. The original channels that were worked—and there are some that are still untouched—were frequently exploited only for their most accessible gold. As soon as widening or deepening channels became too difficult to mine efficiently with the primitive tools available, they were abandoned in favour of more promising locations.

Along with the physical hardships, miners have also had to contend with the host of scoundrels that gold seems to attract. As a commercial venture, the lure of gold can still prove a risky game. The unwary and uninitiated who have dabbled in placer operations on stock markets can attest to that.

For today's recreational panner, however, the possibilities are abundant. Roads and trails continue to open up the backcountry, and with this book as your guide, you'll find the creeks, streams and channels of the Cariboo are by no means played out. Panning for gold is a fascinating, enjoyable and rewarding pursuit. The magic dust, alone or bound up with other minerals and metals, is a beautiful and mysterious substance that displays a different fineness and texture in every creek of the province.

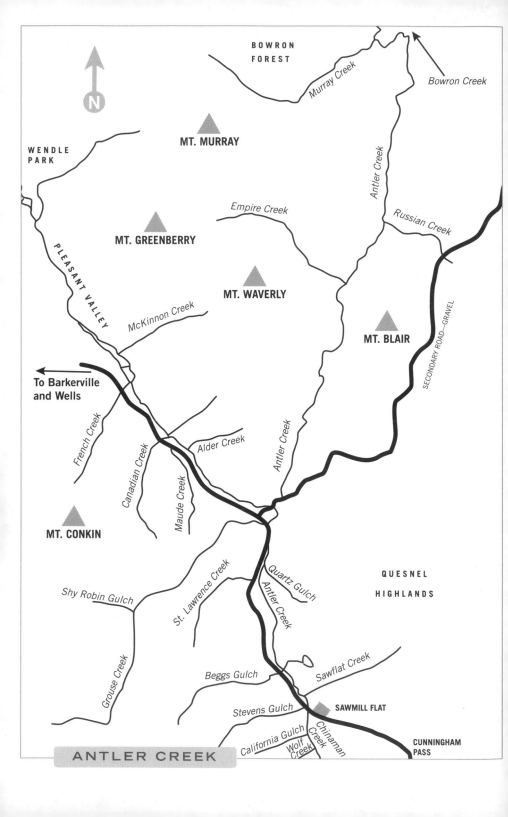

ANTLER CREEK

The headwaters of Antler Creek, located between Mount Burdett and Nugget Mountain, are accessible by road from the town of Wells, east of Quesnel on Highway 26. A main road, secondary roads and hiking trails cross Antler Creek in several places before it flows into the Bowron River below Bowron Lakes. Although access is now relatively easy, many tributaries and promising sections of Antler Creek itself have still not been worked. It's a little-known fact that many of the old, buried channels in the Antler Creek area of the Cariboo have never been mined for their gold.

Antler/Cunningham Creek Pass ✶✶

In 1882 the Yellow Lion Company was operating in the Antler/ Cunningham Creek Pass and found gold on bedrock within a few feet of the surface. Yellow Lion miners traced this find into an old channel in the pass and continued along for about half a kilometre (quarter of a mile), working by hand. The claim paid well. In spite of this success, the company never prospected the next five or six kilometres (three or four miles) of Antler Creek.

Blind Channel ✶

Try prospecting 4 kilometres (2.5 miles) upstream from Antler Creek's mouth on the Bowron River. In 1896 a blind channel was discovered here in the left bank of the creek. This channel was prospected but never mined.

The Ne'er Do Well Dump, Grouse Creek, 1868. CITY OF VANCOUVER ARCHIVES,
AM54-S4-: OUT P906

The discovery of gold on the Quesnel River in 1859 led to major finds on Antler Creek the following year. In 1861, with gold valued at $16 an ounce, Antler Creek was yielding as much as $10,000 a day—$250,000 at today's gold prices.

Sawmill Flat ★

An extensive, ancient high channel is located in this area. Past mining evidence suggests that the old channel, which enriched Antler, leaves the creek's present course on upper Antler Creek. From there it runs through the low pass into Cunningham Creek's valley. In 1901 at the junction of Wolf and Antler Creeks, two one-kilometre (half-mile) leases ran parallel to Antler, south toward Sawmill Flat, and were producing well. An old channel here, high above creek level, has never been mined. Mining records in 1902 also show encouraging results at the lower end of Sawmill Flat.

Chinaman Creek ✶✶

This whole creek is worth prospecting. Chinaman Creek's headwaters lie close to Cunningham Pass. It's a tributary of Wolf Creek, which flows into Antler Creek from the west just below what used to be the Nason claim. There, about half a kilometre (quarter of a mile) and some 60 metres (200 feet) above the Antler Creek valley, Chinaman Creek's old channel was discovered at the turn of the century, and it proved to be one of the most rewarding properties in the area. The channel is about 60 metres (200 feet) wide and about 20 to 25 (70 to 80 feet) high. The whole area still looked to be extremely promising in the 1970s.

Russian Creek ✶✶

A bench nearly a kilometre long and ranging from 150 to 300 metres (500 to 1,000 feet) wide was discovered at the junction of Russian Creek and Antler Creek in 1906. The miners who worked this bench channel found that gold values were increasing with depth, but they never did reach bedrock—where the largest deposits accumulate.

By 1878 several companies had staked claims along the benches of Antler Creek about 16 kilometres (10 miles) downstream from its source. These benches are quite extensive, and the companies that worked them enjoyed good prospects for a number of years.

Construction of the Canadian Pacific Railroad and the lure of a wage drew many miners away from the goldfields in 1885. In 1887 only the Nason Company was working on Antler Creek.

In 1919 very high gold values were found in the Antler Creek bed 19 kilometres (12 miles) north of Barkerville. A dredge was proposed but never built.

The 1921 mining records show that even on well-known creeks there was still plenty of virgin ground. For the next three years, keystone drilling, a method of core sampling, was carried out on Antler Creek and produced great results.

. . . .

In 1950 two small-scale operations were on Antler Creek; upper Antler Creek had just one lease in progress. Lack of machinery limited the size of these operations.

. . . .

From the 1960s to the present not much work has been done on Antler Creek. The biggest obstacle in recent times has been the lack of financing for placer operations.

Grouse Creek ✶

The east bank of Antler Creek, nearly a kilometre upstream from the mouth of Grouse Creek, is another promising area. A small amount of work here yielded sparkling returns in 1908.

Alder Creek ✶

New discoveries were made on upper Antler Creek in 1926. One kilometre from the mouth of Pleasant Valley Creek, prospect Alder Creek's right bank. An old channel was discovered here apparently crossing Alder Creek in a more or less north-to-south direction. On the east side, this old channel is about 36 metres (120 feet) wide and runs south to a point opposite Wolf Creek—where it may once more cross Antler Creek. One kilometre west of this area, on the other side of Alder Creek, the old channel is again exposed. In 1927 water was piped here from China Creek, Wolf Creek and Stevens Gulch, and the channel produced well.

California Gulch ✶

Coarse gold was found on the rim of California Gulch in 1929, but a pre-glacial channel, which starts in the vicinity of Moloney Flat, has never been worked. This channel parallels Antler Creek's present course, joining it between the road and the lower end of China Creek. One kilometre below Sawmill Flat, part of this channel is exposed, but roughly 4 kilometres (2.5 miles) of the channel is still intact—it has never been disturbed. This is located in one of the richest areas of the Cariboo.

In 1932 a private company managed to work the exposed section of the channel where it crosses Antler Creek diagonally, and it paid extremely well. About 79 metres (260 feet) above creek level the bedrock is exposed and the channel lies right next to it. In the early 1970s, the creek portion was staked at this location, but the old channel itself was not. Exploratory panning here produced good results in the bottom 3 metres (10 feet) of the channel, just above creek level.

Men and horses outside the J.H. Todd Co. and the Wake-Up Jake Saloon in Barkerville, 1868. VANCOUVER PUBLIC LIBRARY 8635

Sawflat Creek ✱

A significant discovery was made near the junction of Sawflat Creek and Antler Creek in 1948, when bedrock samples from keystone drilling (core sampling) were examined.

The samples provided conclusive proof that in pre-glacial times Antler Creek, upstream from Sawmill Flat, flowed down the valley of Sawflat Creek and into the Swift River. Like other promising areas in the Antler Creek region, this old channel was prospected, but has never been mined.

HAZARDS

I find in the wintertime you've gotta be a lot more careful when you're prospecting, especially if you're in avalanche country, because I got caught in one once with a snowmobile.

The slide came down, and I didn't see or hear it coming at first because of the noise of the snowmobile. I wasn't looking at the side of the mountain—and all of a sudden it hit me.

Luckily, I went down ahead of the slide, and the snowmobile kept going. I got tossed off it, landed in the snow and kept rolling and trying to run. The chap I was with was ahead of me, maybe by 50 or 60 yards, and he didn't get hit with it, but I did. The snowmobile went one way and I went the other.

I left that snowmobile right there—it was an older model. It was under the snow somewhere. It quit so I couldn't hear it running, and I thought, "To hell with it, let's get outta here before something else comes down."

I never saw that snowmobile again. As far as I know it's still there to this day!

—Jim Lewis

CUNNINGHAM CREEK

The headwaters of Cunningham Creek are located between Yanks Peak and Roundtop Mountain, clearly defined on the topographical map for the top of Quesnel Lake. A review of Cunningham Creek's gold history shows that in spite of its productivity over the years, relatively little work has been done. There are many buried channels in the area. Given the hardships borne by the first prospectors—lack of transport, lack of cabins in the wilderness, lack of financing, lack of water to adequately work claims, lack of machinery—it's not surprising that these buried channels have not been mined out.

Cunningham Creek Pass ✶

In 1888, 4 kilometres (2.5 miles) from Cunningham Creek's mouth, paying gold was found 106 metres (350 feet) up the hillside in the low pass leading to Cunningham Creek. Hand methods were producing 43 grams (1.5 ounces) of gold a day for each man working the area at this time.

Travelling through Cunningham Pass from Antler Creek, the flats are underlain with gravel deposits. In the early 1970s, we made a good living working through there with our old prospecting partner, Pat Harvey. During the dry summer months, using a portable 6-centimetre (2.5-inch) dredge, we were retrieving as much as 400 grams (14 ounces) of gold a day working no more than one metre (three feet) below the surface. In a few places, the pass had previously been prospected, but most of the gravel deposits had never been touched.

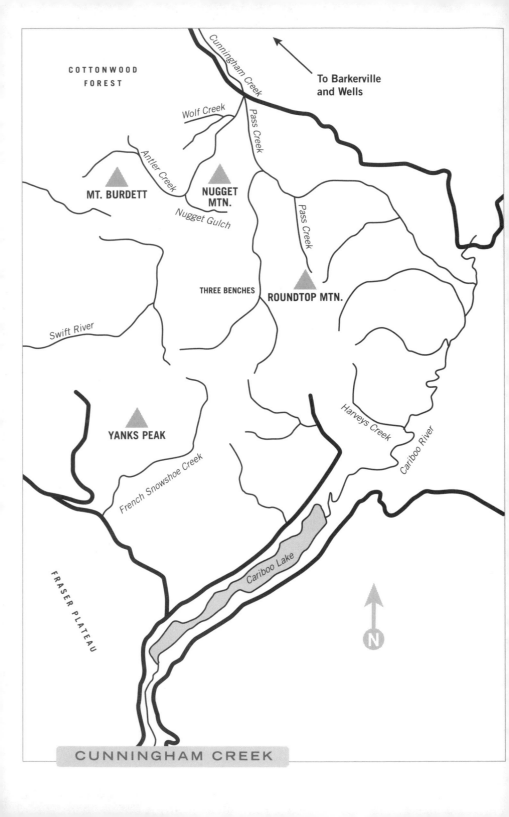

Men at Grouse Claim on Cunningham Creek, 1931. VANCOUVER PUBLIC LIBRARY 9334

Cunningham Channel ★★

There is little doubt that an old channel leads through the low pass into Cunningham Creek's valley. Just below the pass, on the west branch, the creek takes a sharp turn to the east. Here, there's a 12-metre (40-foot) bank of gravel, which proved quite lucrative at the turn of the century. Paying quantities of gold were also found above the west branch, on high benches. The old channel meets creek level six kilometres (four miles) upstream from the west branch. Diggings at this location are relatively shallow; prospecting in more recent times produced results at depths of two metres (six feet).

Old Streambed ★

In 1886 Cunningham Creek's old streambed was discovered 76 metres (250 feet) above creek level, and it produced well. Quartz veins containing gold were also found three kilometres (two miles) west of Roundtop Mountain. A logging road parallels the creek in this location.

There is little record of further mining activity at Pass Creek until 1921, when a small-scale operation was underway on one lease. There was still plenty of virgin ground on many of the well-known placer creeks in the area.

In 1941 hydraulic miners tested a gold-saving device designed to recover gold from black sand. The idea was later tried on the Fraser River south of Quesnel.

The recorded mining history indicates only limited work on Cunningham Creek since the Second World War.

Cunningham Bar ★

At the turn of the century, in an area known as Cunningham Bar (directly east of Nugget Mountain), rich gold deposits were discovered on bedrock. Banks 46 metres (150 feet) high were producing well. Progress was limited to 15 metres (50 feet) a year, however, due to the primitive methods and lack of water for hydraulic mining. In 1907 a dam constructed the previous year burst, halting all work on Cunningham Creek. Prospecting here in the 1970s produced sparkling results in the gravel banks—starting at depths of about one metre (three feet).

Pass Creek ★

An old channel lies in the south side of Cunningham Creek about a kilometre downstream from its confluence with Pass Creek. Records for 1904 show the gold recovered ranged from fine dust to nuggets weighing nine grams (one-third of an ounce). Diggings are relatively shallow at this location.

Nugget Gulch ★

In 1905 a pre-glacial channel was discovered in Nugget Gulch coming in from the head of Cunningham Creek. It's very likely the source of the gold found there. Drilling in 1924 proved up nearly 3 million metres of gravel on Cunningham Pass Creek with good gold values. This was drilled only, never mined.

Old Channel ✴✴

In 1929 Cunningham's old channel was discovered running parallel and west of the existing creek. Both rims of the old channel were well defined, but prospectors failed to trace it to the location where it intersects the present creek. It's believed the channel extends some three kilometres (two miles) downstream from Cunningham's mouth. This area would be well worth exploring.

Three Benches ✴✴

Drilling in 1930 and 1931 yielded unusually good results in three benches located three kilometres (two miles) southwest of Roundtop Mountain, at the confluence of Cunningham and an unnamed creek. On the map you'll see that the road parallels the creek at this location. The first bench was located just a few feet above the creek, the second one 42 metres (140 feet) above creek level, and the third bench is 6 metres (20 feet) higher again. These benches, which appear to be undisturbed by glacial action, are at least 40 metres (130 feet) wide and extend away from the creek for some distance. The benches yielded noteworthy results in 1932 and, a year later, there was new evidence that the old channel tends to run into the right bank of the creek here.

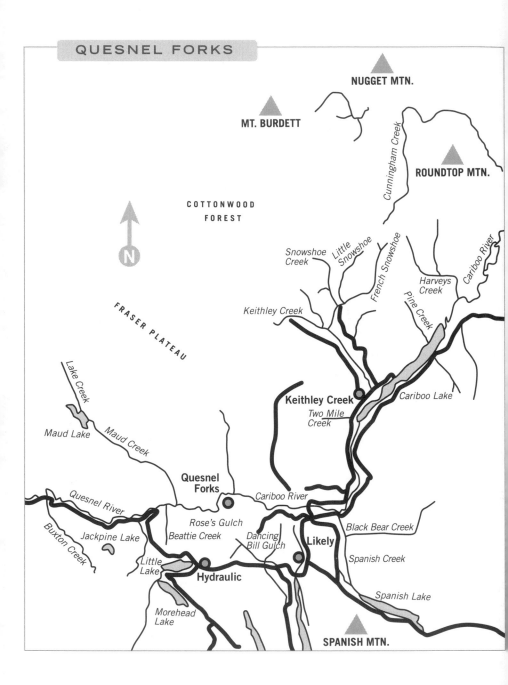

QUESNEL FORKS

NUGGET MTN.

MT. BURDETT

ROUNDTOP MTN.

COTTONWOOD
FOREST

Cunningham Creek

Cariboo River

Snowshoe
Creek

Little
Snowshoe

French Snowshoe

Harveys
Creek

Pine Creek

Keithley Creek

FRASER PLATEAU

Lake Creek

Keithley Creek

Cariboo Lake

Two Mile
Creek

Maud Creek

Maud Lake

Quesnel
Forks

Quesnel River

Cariboo River

Black Bear Creek

Buxton Creek

Jackpine Lake

Rose's Gulch

Beattie Creek

Dancing
Bill Gulch

Likely

Spanish Creek

Little
Lake

Hydraulic

Spanish Lake

Morehead
Lake

SPANISH MTN.

N

QUESNEL FORKS

Just downstream from the town of Likely, for a time in the later part of the 19th century the Quesnel Forks area was almost exclusively a Chinese settlement. Numerous small creeks in the area are rich in possibility, and rich bars have been found all along the south fork from Quesnel Lake. Roads now lead all along the river, and the valley is wide. The surrounding hillsides still contain extensive gold-bearing gravel deposits, 200 metres (700 feet) above the valley floor.

Along with the specific sites mentioned, the following creeks are also known to be gold bearing: Red Gulch Creek, Snowshoe Creek, French Snowshoe Creek, Goose Creek, Duck Creek, Spanish Creek and Cedar Creek.

20 Mile Creek ★★

In 1883 gold was discovered at 20 Mile Creek (west of Buxton Creek toward the Fraser River). At the time there were neither roads nor trails leading into the area, and river travel was a hazardous undertaking because of the river's swift current and many boulders. Prospectors still managed to take excellent returns a few years later. This time the action was on the south side of the Quesnel River, just below 20 Mile Creek. By 1894 there were numerous leases in the area, but little or no work was being performed on them.

In 1875 miners were producing about nine grams (a third of an ounce) a day panning on large benches 50 to 200 feet above the river.

Like Williams Creek, Dancing Bill Gulch is named after Bill Williams, who'd do a little dance every time he found good gold in the pan!

In 1878 very little placer mining was done—most miners were caught up in a mini gold rush, examining hard rock possibilities in the area.

High water meant very little mining was done in 1882, but a dry year in 1883 allowed previously unworked benches to be mined.

High Benches ✷

High Benches is located 10 kilometres (6 miles) above Quesnel Forks on the Cariboo River, cuts in the north side high benches yielded excellent results in 1896. Our own prospecting has shown the river banks at this location are still producing.

Bullion Mine ✷

The Bullion Mine managed by J.B. Hobson came into production in 1897 on an old buried channel on the south fork of the Quesnel River. This channel (see map, page 42) still exists. The Bullion property originally comprised eight leases (180 hectares, or 466 acres) and extended nearly 3 kilometres (2 miles) along the channel's west side. The bars and low benches of the river here have been enriched by a series of crisscrossing channels, some of which have never been mined.

Dancing Bill Gulch ✷

A large gravel deposit follows this small stream to the river, crossing an ancient river channel and exposing gold-bearing gravels. The old channel can be traced for 2 kilometres (1.5 miles) in each direction—nearly paralleling the south fork of the Quesnel River. A rocky ridge, once known as French Bar Bluff, separates the channel and the

J. Likely, John B. Hobson and an unidentified guard beside gold bullion from the Cariboo Hydraulic Mine in Bullion. VANCOUVER PUBLIC LIBRARY 915

river. Upstream from its intersection with Dancing Bill Gulch, this channel turns abruptly into a more recent channel. After crossing this newer channel, the gulch follows it on its turn into the river. Recent dredging and sluicing produced excellent results through here.

Black Jack Gulch ✷

One kilometre southeast of Dancing Bill Gulch, the channel just mentioned crosses Black Jack Gulch. However, this gulch didn't cut deep enough through the rim rock to expose the channel. Gravels we tested here proved rich in gold, ranging from fine dust to nuggets weighing seven grams (a quarter of an ounce). Some of the gold was flattened and well worn; other pieces were in milky white quartz and resembled the vein gold found all over the Cariboo.

Channel Depression ✱✱

To the southeast, this same channel runs in a well-defined depression for about a kilometre until it meets another depression occupied by Little Lake. Little Lake Creek runs west from here, entering Morehead Creek three kilometres (two miles) upstream from the Quesnel River. The course of the old channel should be thoroughly prospected through this area.

Rose's Gulch ✱✱

On the other side of the south fork, along Rose's Gulch, another old channel contains a significant deposit of gold-bearing gravel. Although it was discovered 100 years ago, recent explorations proved this channel is still producing.

Beattie Creek ✱

East of Beattie Creek, on the south bank of the main Quesnel River, a large gravel deposit sits in what's believed to be part of the ancient river system. Gold bearing, this ancient channel runs through a low valley-like depression a kilometre long and ranging from 600 to 900 metres (2,000 to 3,000 feet) wide. We've traced this channel and found it still intact, with paying values.

Morehead Creek ✱

Near the mouth of this creek (10 kilometres, or 6 miles downstream from Quesnel Forks) there's evidence of another huge deposit of gold-bearing gravel in an old river channel. One kilometre upstream from the confluence, gently sloping ground rises on to a steeper line of hills—120 to 150 metres (400 to 500 feet) above the creek. Here, in a depression, Morehead Creek has cut a narrow gulch, and there's a deposit of stratified gravel and gravelly clay that's 600 metres (2,000 feet wide) and 30 to 45 metres (100 to 150 feet) deep. Morehead Creek cut through the bedrock in places and, not far from the western rim, also cut through this stratified deposit, leaving benches of gravel. Without equipment to mine the higher ground, earlier miners were confined to the rich gravels in the creek bed. Our own explorations also revealed evidence of other gold-bearing channels in the area.

Beaver River ✶

At the mouth of Beaver River, west of 20 Mile Creek, mining records note paying ground on high benches on the south side of the Quesnel River. This ground was never fully worked, though, due to labour shortages at the time of discovery. It was consequently still producing paying quantities not long ago.

Block of gold taken from Cariboo Hydraulic Mine in Quesnel Forks, circa 1900.
VANCOUVER PUBLIC LIBRARY 918

Gold recovery device used at the Bullion Mine, circa 1900.
VANCOUVER PUBLIC LIBRARY 919

Lake Creek ✶✶

Lake Creek is a large creek that flows on a steep grade into the head of Maud Lake (previously known as Four Mile Lake). Coarse gold has been found here at a point where the creek's ancient channel is indicated in the left bank. The ground was also worked just downstream from where Lake Creek emerges from a rocky gorge. An ancient buried channel segment, plainly indicated here in the right bank, offers good possibilities.

Maud Creek (Four Mile Creek) ✶✶

Maud Creek meets the Quesnel River six kilometres (four miles) downstream from the Forks. About 1.5 kilometres (1 mile) upstream from here, we've located gold deposits in gravel. These deposits likely emanated from an ancient channel believed to run along the north side of the Quesnel River.

North Bank ✻

Six kilometres (four miles) east of Quesnel Forks, along the north bank of the Cariboo River, a large and thick gravel deposit is exposed by the river. There's good paying gold here as well.

Kangaroo Creek ✻ ✻

Kangaroo Creek flows into the south fork of the Quesnel River one kilometre upstream from the Forks, on the north side. The topography suggests that a pre-glacial channel of considerable length lies buried in the left bank of this creek. Our own prospecting unearthed a remnant of this channel.

Poquette Creek ✻ (not on map)

Poquette Creek cuts through extensive gravel deposits about a hundred metres upstream from its mouth on Quesnel Lake. Likely Gulch, a small tributary of Poquette Creek, flows in from the east 1.5 kilometres upstream and is also worth checking out. A small flume and gravel-washing boxes produced paying values here at one time. Even so, relatively little work was done.

Black Bear Creek ✻

Testing in the valley of this stream, which lies east of Poquette Creek, indicated

In 1912 with the war approaching, there were fewer miners around. Work was proceeding on Spanish Bars and Marten Creeks, however, and Keithley, Goose and Four Mile (Maud) Creeks were being prospected.

Very little mining was done in 1913, but two new areas are mentioned in that year's Ministry of Mines annual report: Honey Creek and Half Mile Gulch.

Around 1901, workings on Spanish Creek recovered as much as 340 grams (12 ounces) of gold every three metres (10 feet).

appreciable gold values. On the north side of Black Bear Creek, earlier sluicing was successful on what appears to be the opening of an old, high channel running into the creek's valley. Old channels are also in evidence along Spanish Creek, which joins Black Bear Creek about 1.5 kilometres (1 mile) south of the Cariboo River.

Keithley Creek *

Keithley Creek flows into Cariboo Lake from the northwest. A channel discovered in the hillside 180 metres (600 feet) above the old creek bed at the turn of the century still exits today. In the 1930s, gold values in gravel were discovered on the left bank of the creek a kilometre upstream from the bridge on the Likely Road. The gravels overlie a rock bed flanking the creek.

Little Snowshoe Creek *

Little Snowshoe Creek is the upper and main tributary of Keithley Creek, which it enters from the northeast. We've prospected extensively through Little Snowshoe Creek, and it's especially rewarding three kilometres (two miles) upstream from its mouth. There, on the left side, an old high channel appears to cut into the hill in a southerly direction.

Upper Pine Creek * *

Gold-bearing gravels were first discovered here in 1935, and the whole area is still excellent, especially the high banks. The creek flows southeast in a narrow V-shaped valley, eventually turning abruptly northeast a kilometre from Cariboo Lake. Here it enters a short canyon, emerges onto bedrock, then flows on for some distance before turning southeast once more to meet the north end of Cariboo Lake.

A glacial moraine a few hundred metres high lies immediately south of the canyon area. Natural features clearly indicate that part of a pre-glacial channel runs under the moraine. A slight depression suggests that its probable course is in a more or less straight line with the canyon.

The local geology also indicates promising bedrock values. Old workings in the vicinity, however, seem to have been directed at post-glacial concentrations on the south side of the creek (north of the pre-glacial channel). Coarse gold was found there.

Harveys Creek ✱

In 1932 prospectors found coarse gold on a gravel bench 8 metres (25 feet) above the creek—on the right bank a short distance upstream from the falls. High values were reported.

Two Mile Creek ✱

Two Mile Creek is a small creek that flows into Cariboo Lake from the west three kilometres (two miles) south of Keithley Creek. It has its source in a small lake known as Two Mile Flat, which extends between Rollie (Duck) Creek and Keithley Creek at an elevation of 100 to 150 metres (350 to 500 feet), above Cariboo Lake. An old channel cuts through Two Mile Creek 2 kilometres (1.5 miles) upstream from its mouth. Segments lie in both banks. The channel is about 4.5 metres (15 feet) wide, and the

In the 1940s, operations on Pine Creek were recovering an average of 23 grams (eight-tenths of an ounce) of gold per metre of washed gravel.

Between 1939 and 1945, with the Second World War in progress, very little mining was done. Aside from the lack of manpower, gold was deemed a non-essential mineral during the war.

Rich gravel deposits remain around Quesnel Forks because highgrading was accepted practice when natural conditions weren't just right. Miners required sufficient water pressure to process gravel through sluices and a grade of at least four percent to wash away the tailings. Even then, gold values had to justify mining costs!

From the 1902 records: "Upon reaching Eureka Creek, early miners fell short of provisions. They felled a tree and hollowed it out to serve as a sluice box—three inches deep and eight inches wide. Shovelling into this improvised sluice, they recovered about 1.5 ounces for each person per day of rough, coarse gold about the size of flaxseed. No doubt a lot of gold escaped due to the crude manner of the improvised box."

downstream section lies in the creek's right bank. Surface testing here produced good results.

These last four creeks are located east of Horsefly and are not on our map, but they are on the same topographic map for Quesnel Lake.

Antoine (Sucker) Creek ✴✴

This creek flows into the Horsefly River five kilometres (three miles) east of Horsefly. In 1929 gold was discovered one kilometre upstream from Antoine Creek's mouth, immediately above a canyon. There's a trail in, and recent sluicing proved that the right bank is productive ground at least a kilometre upstream from here.

MacKay River ✴

Away south of Horsefly Lake, the MacKay River carries gold on all of its bars. At the turn of the century, when the MacKay was known as the South Fork of the Horsefly River, good prospecting is recorded from the mouth of Campbell Creek upstream.

Eureka Creek ✴✴

Eureka Creek was discovered near the headwaters of the South Fork of the Horsefly River (MacKay) in 1902. Panning produced 28 grams (one ounce) a day per man, and good paying gravel was being worked on the south fork as well at the time. This area has never been mined.

Frasergold Creek ★ ★

The discovery of float quartz in Frasergold Creek in the early 1900s suggests that gold washed into the creek from veins in the immediate area. Eureka, Empire (a tributary of Eureka) and Frasergold Creeks are all indicated in the records as relatively shallow—only 60 or 90 centimetres (two or three feet) to bedrock.

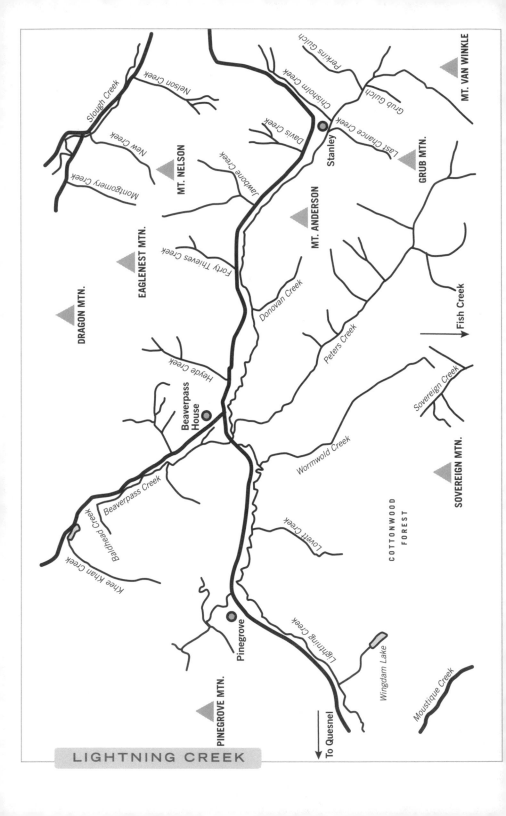

LIGHTNING CREEK

With its headwaters on Mount Agnes, Lightning Creek runs parallel to the Quesnel–Barkerville road (Highway 26) for some distance. The creek and its tributaries have produced gold since the 1860s, and the area continues to be rich in possibility. Lightning Creek still has gold today; a large portion of the creek is staked, though some claims are for sale.

Dunbar Flat ✳✳

In 1896 coarse gold was found on Lightning Creek just above Dunbar Flat near the former settlement of Stanley. It's likely this is an old portion of the Dunbar channel. Working just upstream from the flat and on the higher banks in the area, We've had excellent results with a gold pan and suction dredge. There are good possibilities, too, in a bench that lies 3 metres (10 feet) above the old worked channel. This bench is about 30 metres (100 feet) wide and 300 metres (1,000 feet) long.

Chisholm Creek ✳

Chisholm Creek is a small stream that flows into Lightning Creek at Stanley; its present course is recent in geological terms. The creek has an east and west branch (called Oregon Gulch), and it's believed an old channel ran into this gulch from the south and deposited the auriferous gravels in the area. The channel, now partially covered by a

In 1878 gold was recovered on Lower Lightning Creek about four miles from its confluence with the Swift (or Cottonwood) River.

Moustique Creek produced good results in 1910. Other creeks being worked at that time included Perkins Gulch, Last Chance Creek and Little Valley Creek.

In the 1880s, a large part of Lightning Creek was being held by absentee owners and was not being worked.

Small operations were worked on Devils Canyon (Lake) Creek about eight kilometres (five miles) west of the town of Wells in the 1940s.

hill or slide area identifiable to the south of Chisholm Creek, should be examined. In 1915 Chisholm was producing nuggets weighing as much as 28 grams (1 ounce). The tributary streams flowing in here have produced a lot of gold over the years.

Moustique Creek ✶

This creek is well worth exploring. Moustique Creek has a big pre-glacial channel in the left bank, about a kilometre upstream from its mouth on Lightning Creek. Look for exposed indications of the channel on both rims. This area is noted for coarse nuggets, but fine gold has also been panned here. Gold was first discovered just above the gorge, and the nuggets were found in cracks and crevices as well as in gravels.

Fish Creek ✶✶

A tributary of Sovereign Creek, Fish Creek appears to contain an old buried channel, which could be an upstream extension of the Moustique Creek channel. Lovette Creek was also likely enriched by this same channel.

Perkins Gulch ✶✶

This is another tributary of Lightning Creek that displays strong indications of a productive old channel. We've been well rewarded prospecting through here.

Last Chance Creek ✶✶

A kilometre up from its source, Last Chance Creek has produced nuggets weighing more than 28 grams (1 ounce). A pre-glacial channel lies in the right bank of this creek. In 1932 superficial diggings clearly showed that the modern creek cuts into the old channel at certain points. The rich returns suggested that gold from the ancient channel was being reconcentrated on the bedrock of the modern creek. Working this area in more recent times provided glittering proof of ongoing deposits.

Lover's Leap ✶

Near Lover's Leap (marked by provincial sign on Highway 26) a large bench area is still intact. There's evidence of a high channel crossing Lightning Creek in a northwest-southeast direction here. The channel's continuation northwest of the road is clearly defined by a valley of meadows. In a gulch on the right bank of Lightning Creek—immediately adjacent to the road and about 45 metres (150 feet) down—fairly coarse gold was found in glacial gravels overlying rock. Lack of water for hydraulic mining in the early 1930s hindered work here.

Devils Canyon ✶

Farther east on the Quesnel–Barkerville road, Devils Canyon was the site of a new discovery in 1938. Meadowlands are located on both sides of the Chisholm Creek/Devils Lake Divide, and the discovery was made at a meadow on the north end of the canyon, upstream from old workings. Earlier miners had concentrated their efforts on the post-glacial deposits above the east wall of Devils Canyon.

Devils Canyon, 1886. CITY OF VANCOUVER ARCHIVES, AM54-S4-1-: CVA 4-35

Beaver Pass ✷

A wide valley, Beaver Pass deserves close inspection of both its tributaries in the pass and of the region beyond the north end of Ahbau Lake. For years gold was recovered from the creeks around here. Good returns obtained by prospectors working by hand in 1932 sparked renewed interest in the area. There are known concentrations of gold on the bedrock and false bedrock of the creeks—many of which occupy post-glacial channels. The streambeds cross pre-glacial channels, which in several places are plainly indicated, lying buried on one side or the other of the existing creeks.

Baldhead and Khee Khan Creeks ✷✷

A similar situation exists along Baldhead Creek and Khee Khan Creek, both of which run into Beaver Pass just north of Four Mile Lake. These creeks have cut through old channels of gold-bearing gravel and have reconcentrated the gold on their creek beds. It seems likely that some of these channels are native to the Beaver Pass (Bedrock) valley and that the placer material is of local origin. At one point, Baldhead Creek flows along bedrock on the right rim of an ancient channel. This channel is buried in the left bank of the creek, and the area has produced fairly coarse, well-worn gold.

Owing to the general hard times and scarcity of other work during the First World War, many placer miners were forced back to creeks the "Old Timers" said were worked out. Luckily, though, many of these so-called worked-out creeks proved once again to be lucrative.

No Name Creek ✶

In 1938 a new discovery was made 6 kilometres (3.5 miles) up from Beaver Pass House. Coarse gold on true bedrock was found a couple of metres below clay on No Name Creek, which flows into Beaver Pass from the northeast, north of Baldhead Creek.

Ground sluicing was done in the 1930s on Kwong Foo Creek, which runs parallel to Slade Creek, about 300 metres (1,000 feet) away.

Gagen Creek ✶

Gagen Creek flows into Lightning Creek from the south, near Coldspring House. At 2 kilometres (1.5 miles) upstream from the confluence, a new discovery in 1932 turned up spectacular gold in the right bank of Gagen Creek. Look for an area where rock appears near the creek's surface and frequent outcrops are seen. The bench ground along here is only a couple of metres above the creek and was so rich that 1,049 grams (37 ounces) of gold were obtained from about 250 metres (275 yards) of gravel.

Below this point the creek has deepened its bed and the benches for a kilometre run to a width of 60 metres (200 feet), offering good possibilities. The higher banks in this area are also productive. In recent times, we've found coarse gold, fairly worn, in cracks and crevices as well as in gravels. Gagen Creek eventually enters Lost Valley and flows northwest to its junction with Lightning Creek.

Two Channels ✶✶

Two channels cross Lightning Creek in the bench region just described. These channels are roughly a kilometre apart. One is the valley through which the upper portion of Gagen Creek flows; the other is Lost Valley. Lost Valley is dry, but is clearly defined and more than 550 metres (600 yards) wide nearing Lightning Creek.

RIVALRIES

There was this one chap who had the great habit of telling me that he was going to stake me in—meaning that if I was staking mining claims, he was gonna come along and by the time I got my first claim done he would have all the rest in the area staked.

And he was always buggin' me about this. So it became not exactly adversarial, but it became sort of a "Well if you're in an area, I know it's good, so I'm gonna be in there too, and I'm gonna get anything I can before you get it all" sort of thing.

And this went on for a few years.

One day just before Christmas, one of my prospecting partners and I knew claims were coming up at midnight that night. That was the anniversary date.

So we went out at about 8 o'clock figuring we'd be on the ground at midnight. This used to be a common trick years ago—go in at midnight and start your staking, and by 9 o'clock in the morning you're in the recorder's office recording the claim.

We took a third guy with us. The other chap that was always with me, he had bought himself four bottles of rye for Christmas and I think a bottle of gin or something. It was likely his liquor supply for the whole winter because he didn't drink that much. So we drove out and came to a fork in the road, and all of a sudden we see vehicle tracks ahead of us in the fresh snow.

Well I knew there was a cabin just down the road from the claims that we wanted. "We're in trouble now," I said. "There's somebody else in here probably got the same idea as us, gonna stake these at midnight."

So we drove in a little ways farther and when I got about a quarter of a mile away from the cabin I shut the truck off. I'd shut the lights off before that because, with the snow, there was enough visibility. We get up close to the cabin, and I see a red Ford there, which I recognized immediately as belonging to this guy that was always buggin' me and saying he was gonna stake me in!

So I walked back to the pickup and told the guys what was going on. And I'm trying to think of what I can do, because if we drive by with our 4×4 they're gonna spot us immediately.

So I said to the older chap: "Can I borrow two bottles of rye from you . . . until tomorrow, when we go back to town?" He looked at me like, what did I want two bottles of rye for?

"Well I'd like to borrow them until tomorrow!" I said. "I'll replace them in the morning."

"Well okay," he said.

Then I turned to the third chap—and this third one he was a real drunk, he really got into it—and I said to him: "I want you to take your rifle and packsack and knock on the door of that cabin and tell 'em you've been hunting, that you stayed out too long in the bush and that you'd like to stay the night. Produce one bottle of rye," I said, "but don't produce both of them immediately."

And I told him to be on the road the next morning by 7 o'clock, otherwise he'd be walking out. "Now don't you go and get loaded. Make sure you give them more than you take yourself when you pour the drinks. And you pour it! You load their cups up good and keep yours light."

Well, this worked. When the other chap and I drove by at about 11 o'clock that night we could hear the laughing and the hootin' and the hollerin', and we went in and we staked the claims.

Next morning I see this chap and he's sittin' on the side of the road with his head in his hands. "Jeez, I sure could use a drink," he says.

Well, we had about a 16-mile drive to town and we got in too early for him because the beer parlours weren't open yet or anything and we had to sit around for a while. But as soon as the mining recorder opened I was in there recordin' those claims immediately. About a week later I ran into the two guys from the cabin on the street. "How's the staking in business?" I said.

And the one guy that was always buggin' me, he said: "You dirty sonofabitch. You sent him in there to get us pissed didn't you?"

And I said: "I didn't do anything!"

And he said: "No, no, no! We figured it out . . . We followed his trail out and we saw where he got back in your pickup."

And I said: "Well, that's one time you got staked in!"

Well, they didn't like it. I mean, I guess they were pretty angry the next morning, but they just took it all in good stride.

—Jim Lewis

WILLOW RIVER

Willow River, renowned for deep ground and buried channels, drains the largest area of rich placer ground in the Cariboo. Williams Creek—which runs through the heart of historic Barkerville—and Jack of Clubs Creek together form the river's east fork. Both merge with the Willow River at Wells. The river's west fork, once known as Lost Creek, is now named Slough Creek. Its confluence with the river lies 11 kilometres (7 miles) west of Wells on the opposite side of Island Mountain.

The Willow River has immense gravel banks and almost every tributary ever prospected has produced paying gold, especially the creeks entering from the east side. Still, opportunities abound beyond the sites mentioned on Hardscrabble Creek, Sugar Creek, Tregillus Creek and Rucheon Creek.

Big Valley Creek ✶

Lying northwest of Barkerville, Big Valley Creek has its source in Nine Mile Lake. The creek runs for kilometres through a broad valley that ranges from 150 to 300 metres (500 to 1,000 feet) wide. Plenty of gold has been found close to the valley's surface, and it still shows excellent potential. There's a canyon eight kilometres (five miles) downstream from the source, below which the valley narrows to 120 metres (400 feet). Below the canyon, miners were enjoying good prospects at the turn of the century, but work halted abruptly in

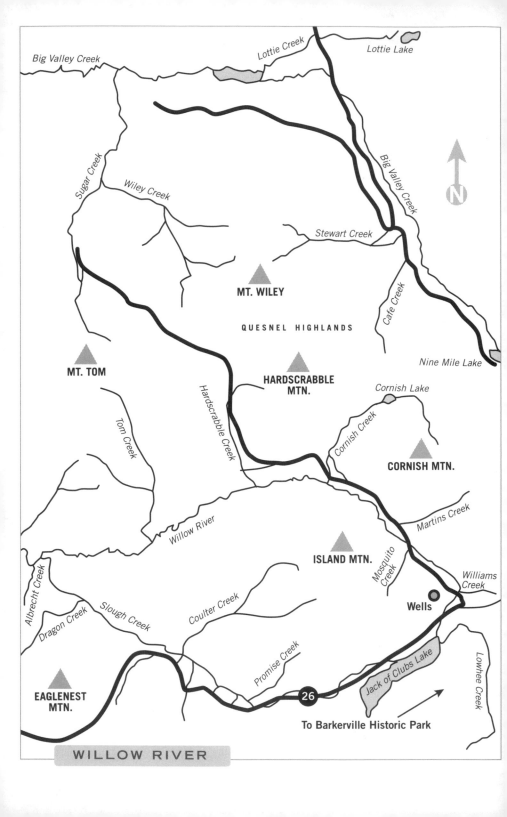

Two gold bricks from the Cariboo Gold Quartz Mine in Wells, circa 1903.
VANCOUVER PUBLIC LIBRARY 1817

the face of high water. The tributaries flowing in from the south—Cafe, Stewart and Sugar Creeks—have all been productive and there's no question that an immense amount of gold-bearing gravel is located in this area.

Devils Lake Creek ✶

This is another area that was never worked thoroughly in earlier times because of a lack of water for hydraulic mining. Past records suggest there were two distinct runs of gold—one running up Devils Lake Creek, the other running roughly parallel to Slough Creek.

Slough Creek ✶✶

Slough Creek is a relatively small stream running through a flat-bottomed valley. From along its southern tributaries—Nelson, Burns and New Creeks—a lot of gold was taken in the early 1900s. A bench of paying gravel extends

In 1876 two companies were prospecting Carry On Creek, a tributary of the Willow River.

Cafe Creek was being prospected and developed for mining in 1903. Stewart Creek was averaging 70 to 85 grams (2.5 to 3 ounces) of gold for every 3 metres (10 feet) worked.

Burns Creek, Slough Creek, Dragon Creek and Coulter Creek were being worked on a steady basis in 1912, but conditions were dry, and hydraulic and sluice operations required massive amounts of water to wash the high banks.

On McCarters Gulch, Conklin Gulch and Hardscrabble Creek, prospecting was good in 1899. Another tributary, Cornish Creek, produced gold in shallow ground near its source.

In 1901 mining tunnels were driven in with some success, but flooding kept driving back the miners.

Northeast of Barkerville, the Bear and Goat Rivers were prospected and hold great promise.

along the south side of the valley, and an old channel runs south toward Lightning Creek.

Mosquito Creek ✶

Not to be confused with Moustique Creek, Mosquito Creek is rather unusual: gold values have been found higher up—on the rim rock—rather than on bedrock. Although it's a short creek that flows into the Willow River only 2 kilometres (1.5 miles) northwest of Wells, plenty of paying ground had still not been worked by 1914, despite the rich gravels.

Albrecht Creek ✶✶

Located three kilometres (two miles) downstream from Dragon Creek, Albrecht Creek has an intriguing history. In the early 1900s, a prospecting tunnel was driven into the banks to tap into a channel that was previously discovered in the hillside. The principal owner of the only area being worked by 1906 was struck by a fatal illness and the property was shut down, despite the fact results were improving as the work progressed.

Dragon Creek ✶✶

An old channel crosses Dragon Creek a kilometre upstream from its mouth. The channel parallels the Willow River for 26 kilometres (16 miles), running in a slightly more westerly direction, before turning east and meeting the river. This is believed to be the old channel of Lost Creek (later renamed Slough Creek). From knowledge gained at the Dragon Creek exposure and from other prospecting evidence, it's believed this channel crosses Tregillus Creek. The channel is likely the source of gold found in Rucheon and Baldhead Creeks, and the rich spots in the right bank of Tregillus Creek. From here to the point 16 kilometres (10 miles) north where it meets the Willow River, the old channel is well defined.

Archer and Deadtimber Creeks ✱✱

Archer and Deadtimber Creeks empty into the Willow River north of Tregillus Creek and cut through the same channel. Both creeks have been worked successfully upstream, and it's more than likely that the old channel is the source of their gold.

Ahbau Creek ✱

Located between Lodi Lake and Ahbau Lake, Ahbau Creek is still productive, even though it has surrendered plenty of gold over the years. All the creeks draining from the west into Ahbau Creek have paid good dividends from surface work. Judging from recent prospecting in the area, it is still promising.

Aura Fina Creek ✱✱

In 1951 work started on a new area above

Larsen Gulch, off Rucheon Creek, was worked in 1943 with pleasing results for a small-scale operation.

Shepherd Creek, Hardscrabble Creek and Grouse Creek were all giving good returns for the amount of work done. According to the Ministry of Mines, "Each year, high water rushes down more auriferous gravels and more gold is deposited in the streambeds. People have been known to profitably work the same portion of the creek bed for 10 years or more."

In 1941 labour for mining was frozen, gold being a nonessential war mineral. Consequently placer mining slowed to a minimum during the war years.

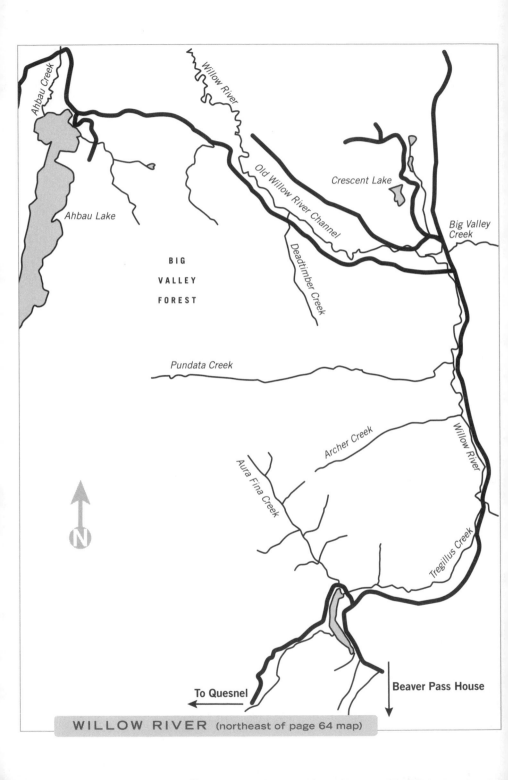

Ahbau Creek

Willow River

Old Willow River Channel

Crescent Lake

Big Valley Creek

Ahbau Lake

BIG VALLEY FOREST

Deadtimber Creek

Pundata Creek

Archer Creek

Willow River

Aura Fina Creek

Tregillus Creek

N

To Quesnel

Beaver Pass House

WILLOW RIVER (northeast of page 64 map)

the canyon on Aura Fina Creek after evidence of an ancient channel was discovered on the west bank. The canyon is 2 kilometres (1.5 miles) upstream from Tregillus Creek.

Old Willow River Channel ✷✷

The Willow River in pre-glacial times used to occupy a channel a kilometre or more east of its present position. Glacial drift (the George Creek glacier) blocked this former channel and forced the river into several different courses to the west until, eventually, it cut the bed it now occupies. The pre-glacial channel lies mainly to the east, and the rock benches there expose the successive channels occupied by the river.

Lowhee Creek and Mine ✷✷

Until it shut down in 1947, the Lowhee Mine was the oldest continuously operated placer mine in the Cariboo. Lowhee Creek has been extremely productive in the past, yet ground was left untouched between the mine and Stouts Gulch.

The Mucho Oro Gold Mining Company, Lowhee Creek, 1868.

Coulter Creek ✶

Try working a kilometre upstream from Coulter Creek's mouth. Look for signs of a buried channel on the north side about 9 metres (30 feet) above creek level.

Despite encouraging returns from prospecting on Coulter Creek, no serious mining was undertaken. The Eight Mile Lake area also showed promise in the creek beds

Williams Creek ✶

As early as 1876, an area just above Mink Gulch was being successfully mined, though more attention was being paid to the east bank of Williams Creek. In the early 1900s, a blind channel about 12 metres (40 feet) wide was discovered and its walls were recorded as 9 metres (30 feet) high. Despite intense interest from the onset of the Cariboo Gold Rush, in 1932 a productive new portion of the creek was discovered opposite Mink Gulch. Williams Creek is today still attracting lots of interest from small companies and individual prospectors.

Records from 1904 say that Williams Creek had been continuously worked for 44 years—but only over a 4-kilometre (2.5-mile) section.

In 1952 Conklin Gulch and Emory Gulch, tributaries of Stouts Gulch, were hydraulic mined on a small scale.

Stouts Gulch ✶

Very rich ground, again overlooked by previous miners, was found on Stouts Gulch in 1913. A tributary of Stouts Gulch— Emory Gulch—also produced excellent results at that time. These last two examples, both in popular areas that are now part of a historic park, illustrate how easy it is to miss paying ground—even when it's right under your nose!

HIXON CREEK

Hixon Creek joins the Fraser River about 56 kilometres (35 miles) south of Prince George. First prospected in the late 1800s, the creek underwent exploration of placer ground beginning just before the turn of the century. Records indicate that by 1935, none of the pre-glacial channels on Hixon Creek had been touched. The next mention of Hixon Creek is 1948, when only one lease was under production. Since then, surprising as it may seem, there's been little recorded interest in the area.

Bedrock Values ✶✶

Hixon Creek gravels overlay a band of white clay, which can easily be mistaken for bedrock. Don't be fooled. Coarse gold has been found in this clay to a depth of a few metres. Along Hixon Creek and its tributaries, good paying gold has been found on bedrock, on false bedrock and in the high benches. Just downstream from its confluence with Government Creek, placer gold was found right on the surface of Hixon Creek in 1922.

Hixon Creek Falls ✶

About a kilometre upstream from its confluence with Government Creek, 27-metre (90-foot) falls descend in three steps. Beyond the falls, for several kilometres upstream, wire gold veins in quartz pieces have been found. Within an area of 4 square metres (40 square feet)

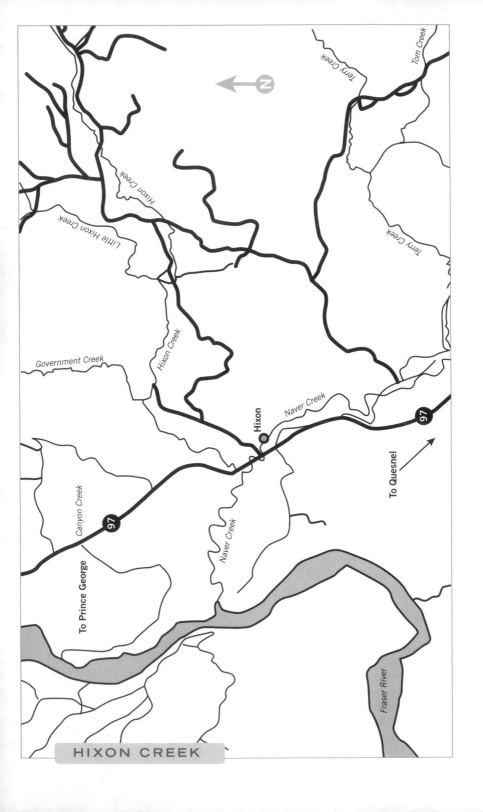

HIXON CREEK

miners recovered $500 in gold when prices were $17 per ounce. They only worked the surface to a depth of about a metre. We've prospected claims here fairly recently (for their owners) and the results were excellent. Mining records for 1927 indicate that a large bench—137 metres (450 feet) long and 91 metres (300 feet) wide—is located farther upstream and at that time had still to be prospected.

Old Channel ✶✶

Upstream from the falls, a pre-glacial channel appears to run along the north side of Hixon Creek for about 6 kilometres (3.5 miles). The channel eventually cuts across to the south side of the creek somewhere below the falls.

Low Bench ✶

In 1931 a spectacular new discovery was made on Hixon Creek. You can see that most of the creek's left bank above the falls sits on a low-lying bench. Miners recovered more than 2,097 grams (74 ounces) of gold from only a small yardage of gravel here. And they did it while shovelling gravel over their heads to reach the height necessary to work the sluices!

Government Creek ✶✶

Along with its tributaries, this area is highly recommended. The whole watershed, which follows a southerly course to its confluence with Hixon Creek, was overlooked for many years. In 1915 enterprising prospectors at work on Government Creek found coarse, heavy gold and nuggets weighing more than 28 grams (1 ounce). Similar gold values have since been found 3 kilometres (2 miles) upstream from the confluence, at a point where gravel and clay banks rise 30 to 45 metres (100 to 150 feet) above creek level. Although some of the gold found here was fine, there was almost no evidence of flour

In 1949 and 1950, only one lease was worked at Low Bench, the balance of the area being largely ignored.

Starting in the 1950s, frequent conflict arose between mineral-title holders and placer-claim holders. This limited exploration of Government Creek.

In 1954 one miner recorded a small amount of sluicing on Government Creek; on Hixon Creek, only one lease area was being worked.

Slides and floods stopped most work on Little Hixon Creek in 1962; by 1965 work had resumed but was soon halted because of a shortage of water.

gold. This suggests that the gold originated locally. We've prospected this area and found that black sand is also present, along with limited values in platinum.

Canyon Creek ✶ ✶

A large stream that follows a wide valley west until, 32 kilometres (20 miles) upstream, it runs through a canyon for 8 kilometres (5 miles). In 1930 gold was discovered at the lower end of the canyon where the valley opens out again. Coarse nuggets turned up in the river bed and gravel banks near a bench roughly 150 metres (500 feet wide). The low benches on both sides of the creek also held coarse, placer gold. From here the creek runs north in a wide, flat-bottomed valley until it reaches the Fraser River.

Little Hixon Creek ✶

Also known as the north fork of Hixon Creek, Little Hixon Creek is well worth exploring. In 1932 very coarse gold and nuggets weighing as much as 113 grams (4 ounces) were found about 400 metres upstream from its confluence with Hixon Creek. A shortage of water for sluicing and subsequent legal problems suspended work on the creek. We've prospected here, and it's likely an ancient channel segment is located in this area.

Terry Creek ★★

Coarse gold and large quartz rocks have been found on Terry Creek. Upstream, immediately above Tom Creek, low-lying benches of auriferous gravels line both banks. The valley here is between 150 and 275 metres (500 and 900 feet) wide. Farther on, the creek runs through a rocky gorge for some distance. Five kilometres (three miles) upstream from Tom Creek, it enters a canyon for 274 metres (300 yards), above which the valley widens again. At its upper end, the canyon's walls are 27 metres (90 feet) high, and a clearly defined channel runs northwest toward Hixon Creek.

A 1967 slide of overburden into the mining area stopped the recovery of gold until the debris could be cleared.

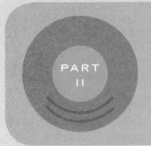

PART II

SOUTHWESTERN BC, VANCOUVER ISLAND AND HAIDA GWAII

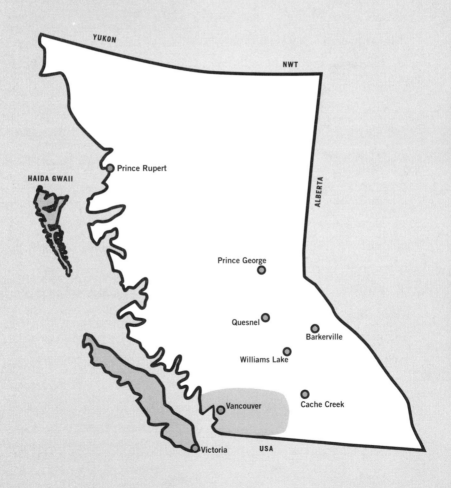

YUKON

NWT

ALBERTA

Prince Rupert

HAIDA GWAII

Prince George

Quesnel

Barkerville

Williams Lake

Cache Creek

Vancouver

Victoria

USA

....

BEYOND HOPE

Hard nuggets of historical fact, like so many easy fortunes, can slip away before anyone notices. Sometimes there's a clear road of events, a definitive record. Other times, the winding trail to the past is muddied by a lacework of crisscrossing tracks and competing claims. Take the first gold strike in BC—that obscure stuff of legend—and you'll see the way back offers several inviting turns.

One account had Donald McLean, chief trader of the Hudson's Bay Company, purchasing gold from the Shuswap people as early as 1855, when he was appointed factor of Fort Kamloops. McLean later moved to Hat Creek and ran a road house there for a time before meeting his fate on an excursion into the Chilcotin . . . but that's another story.

George B. McCellan sparked a flurry of excitement when he discovered gold on the Similkameen River around the same time. As for the Thompson and Fraser watersheds, well, popular lore says a Native man from the Lytton area chanced upon the first nugget while stooping for a drink of water in the Nicomen River in 1856. There are likely other tales, too.

One fact remains clear and beyond dispute: by 1858 word was out about some spectacular gold finds in the colony of British Columbia, and the Cariboo gold rush was underway. Over the next 25 years the gold strikes of the Cariboo and Cassiar areas drew thousands of eager prospectors to the central regions of BC.

In the feverish rush northward, the lower Fraser River and its tributary creeks were largely passed over until the mid-1880s. But those who did hang around to try their luck were well rewarded. By official accounts, Hills Bar alone produced more than $2 million in placer gold during the 1860s and 1870s. How much more of the precious metal slipped into the poles and went unreported is a matter of speculation, secrecy being a miner's best friend—as essential to the mystique as a sixth sense for the flash spots.

From Chilliwack all the way to its confluence with the Thompson River at Lytton, the rolling Fraser has revealed itself time and again as a river of glittering prospects, a surging force that continues to deposit gold dust in its bars and in its banks. Plenty of creeks and streams run by the quartz veins of the surrounding mountains and all eventually feed into the Fraser's churning waters. This combination of raw power and wild promise earned the Fraser a deserved reputation, which was further fuelled by Dr. George Dawson, an early prospector, who coined an enduring description of the river as "a giant sluice box" containing untold millions in gold.

Because of the river's grinding flow, the Fraser's placer has a distinctive, fine texture. This fine gold can be a bit trickier to recover, and fish oil from spawning salmon poses an added challenge in season because it binds up fine gold. Be sure to check any fish oil floating in back eddies! Keep in mind that there are plenty of bright prospects away from the river itself, especially in the deposits of gravel that line both banks, sometimes far above the high-water mark. Where you can get to them, these high banks are well worth the added effort since they've never received the close attention paid to other areas.

In the early days of mining when interest was at its peak, conditions were harsh, transportation was poor, tools were primitive and pumps generally weren't up to the pressure demands of higher ground. It's easy to see why many productive areas were all but ignored. In a time of gold fever, your typical miner, eager for quick profits, would put serious effort only into the easiest, most accessible, high-grade sites. And there always seemed to be something a bit more promising just around the bend.

Amid all this bustle and activity, speculation was rampant. Reports from the Fraser River and Siwash Creek between 1880 and 1890 make frequent mention of leaseholds never developed by their lessees. To quote from the mining records: "In the majority of instances, they were merely obtained for speculative purposes, frequently irrespective of their value as mining properties, with the object of disposing of the rights for a considerable amount. When this experiment failed, the rents remained unpaid and the leases were allowed to lapse."

So it goes: placer leases are still taken out and retained in the roguish hope of flipping them to an unwary buyer. As with other avenues of life, the time-honoured rule here is *caveat emptor*—buyer beware. Thoroughly prospect any site that piques your interest before investing.

Prospecting the Fraser's banks near Yale, 1870s.

Sternwheeler *Lillooet* at Yale, 1865.

That said, be assured that there's still plenty of placer gold around. Poor access, basic tools and short seasons all hampered mining efforts of the past. Roads and trails continue to open up the back country, and the rich gravel banks skirting the upper reaches of the Fraser River continue to be undermined by the roaring spring floods, which scour away new deposits and carry them downstream to lodge in some faraway nook, bar or bank of the river. Today's recreational panner will find that the old sites keep producing and the overlooked gems, well, they're out there still. Very little mining or placer exploration has occurred in the last 40 years. Be that as it may, the general locations described on pages 10 to 14 as best suited to deposits of float (placer gold) can be worked every year, always with anticipation, sometimes with striking results.

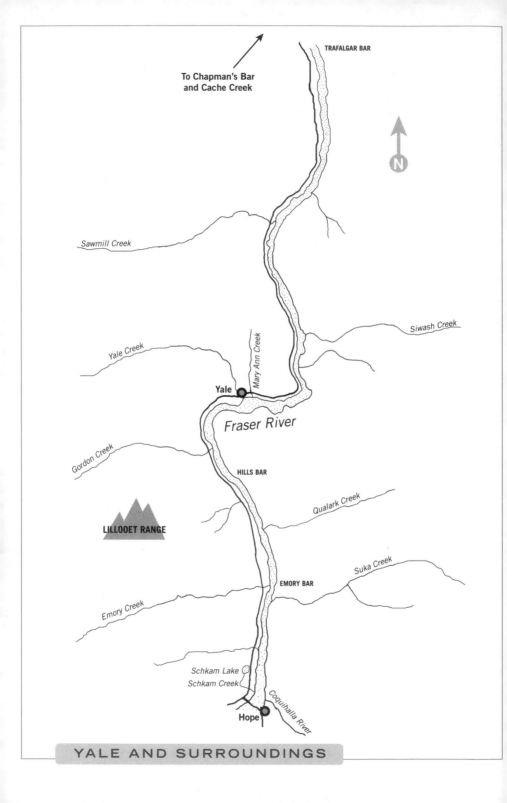

To Chapman's Bar
and Cache Creek

TRAFALGAR BAR

N

Sawmill Creek

Siwash Creek

Mary Ann Creek

Yale Creek

Yale

Fraser River

Gordon Creek

HILLS BAR

LILLOOET RANGE

Qualark Creek

Suka Creek

EMORY BAR

Emory Creek

Schkam Lake
Schkam Creek

Coquihalla River

Hope

YALE AND SURROUNDINGS

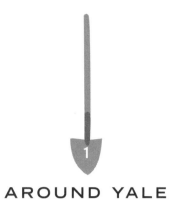

AROUND YALE

A historic town on the west side of the Fraser River north of Hope, Yale was the uppermost limit for 19th-century paddlewheelers travelling upriver from the coast. A rocky section just upstream from the town blocked all further passage. Droves of eager miners disembarked here to continue their journey north on foot with pack horses and mules. From the 1860s on, Yale was a booming, bustling place. Though quieter today, the main road runs right through town, and there are plenty of access points to the river.

Hills Bar ✶

Early placer interest on the Fraser concentrated in two areas: at the end of Hills Bar flat, just south of Yale, and at Union Bar flat some eight kilometres (five miles) farther downstream. Flats extend along both sides of the Fraser here, and the bars and banks of this historic area continue to be enriched by fine gold.

In the mid-1890s, excellent returns were still being reported from Hills Bar flats, and several groups working the Fraser's banks and bars near Yale were enjoying the best results there in years.

"The golden harvest is perennial," observed the 1895 mining records. Hills Bar looked even richer in 1896, though many leases were idle because of high water.

Word of this ongoing success spread, so that by 1899 several companies had staked new claims at Hills Bar. A succession of hard

A find on Hills Bar in 1858 sparked a rush that saw more than 30,000 men. As local minister Reverend Lundin described it, "Never in the migrations of men has been seen such a rush so sudden and vast."

In 1876 Chinese miners reported good returns working the banks of Hills Bar flat by hand. By 1885 most miners on the Fraser River upstream from Yale and Hope were Chinese. They focused mostly on the bars and banks across the river from Yale, and upstream between Yale and Lytton.

Access to Siwash Creek has always been a challenge. In 1897 only minimal assessment work was done here to keep existing claims in good standing. Just upstream from Siwash Creek, Five Mile Creek and Eight Mile Creek were producing well.

seasons limited their operations, however, and mining in general declined in the years leading up to and during the First World War.

The few people still working the area continued to reap the benefits of their labours, though, and when the war ended in 1918, the mining recorder's office was flooded with new inquiries about the availability of claims between Hope and Yale. By the late 1920s, interest had again tapered off and has never resumed to the same degree.

Siwash Creek ✶✶

Entering the Fraser about a kilometre upstream from Yale on the other side of the river, Siwash Creek was prospected as early as 1875. In contrast to the fine gold of the Fraser, the placer in Siwash Creek is coarse, and there are frequent deposits of quartz laced with gold stringers. Indications of an old gold-bearing channel are visible five kilometres (three miles) upstream from the creek's mouth. Placer gold has also been recovered from the north, middle and south forks for Siwash Creek.

According to the 1893 records, "The character of gold recovered from alluvial claims on Siwash Creek, together with excellent samples of gold-bearing quartz, indicate that free [placer] gold is plentiful."

Chinese miners washing gold in the Fraser River Canyon, 1870s.

The creek's headwaters run through gold-bearing quartz veins. Assayed at the turn of the century, these veins showed 283 grams (10 ounces) per ton—a striking figure. To put it in perspective, hardrock mining has been considered a worthwhile venture when an assay shows as little as 21 grams (three-quarters of an ounce) per ton. Most of the early gold found on Siwash Creek overlay bedrock—in the creek itself and in the banks—yet very little placer mining was recorded along it from 1900 on.

By 1921 the earlier placer claims had reverted back to the government and were again open for new staking. In spite of this, only limited prospecting is recorded thereafter. Our own explorations through here in 1996 proved that Siwash still yields bright colours in every pan.

In 1915 a slide blocked Siwash Creek. A huge backlog of water had to be drained before any work could continue, as there was no way to dispose of the washed gravel.

Schkam Creek ✳

Located a kilometre north of Hope on the west side of the Fraser, Schkam Creek is another good prospect. Miners working the top gravels at the mouth of the creek in 1932, when it was called Johnson Creek, discovered a large amount of fine gold. This placer accumulation was a new run, unseen before, concentrated from the glacial moraines along the Fraser River. The find kept miners busy late into the season, and they profited well from rockers and worked around large boulders.

Other Bright Spots

Numerous other sites are worth exploring, especially the areas in and around the mouths of creeks flowing into the Fraser River.

Suka Creek

Opposite the former townsite of Emory, miners found coarse gold in 1899 on what was then known as Cascade Creek. They did well with only basic tools.

Emory Bar

A placer mining training camp was established around Emory Bar in the early 1930s, encouraging people to learn the prospecting trade.

Trafalgar Bar

About 16 kilometres (10 miles) north of Yale, near Spuzzum, the gravels at river level as well as higher up in the banks at Trafalgar Bar have a productive history.

Chapman's Bar

Nineteen kilometres (12 miles) north of Yale, across the Alexandra Bridge to Chapman's Bar, this location has plenty of worthwhile sites including ground well above the present river's course. Gold-bearing gravel at one time was sent 27 metres (90 feet) down a chute here for washing in the river.

Yale Creek

Yale Creek flows into the Fraser at the townsite and has produced coarse gold from both its bed and its banks. A road follows the creek's course for some distance, and a silver claim is located upstream.

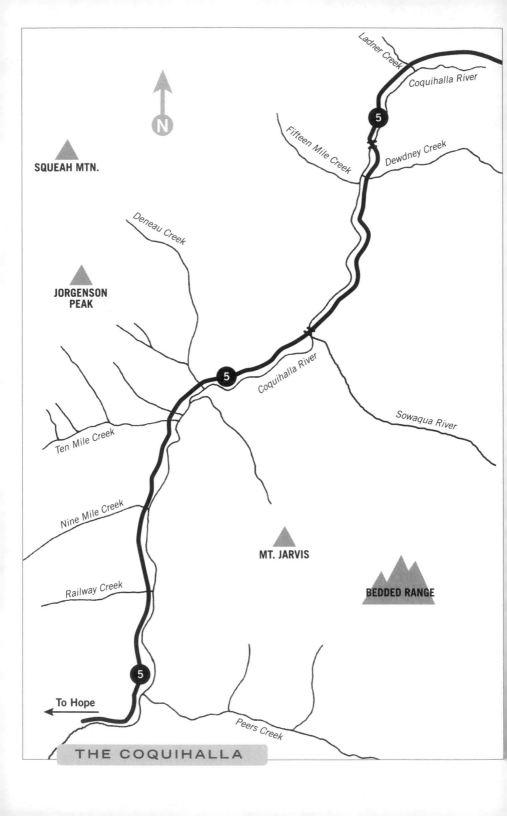

Ladner Creek

Coquihalla River

5

Fifteen Mile Creek

Dewdney Creek

SQUEAH MTN.

Deneau Creek

JORGENSON
PEAK

5

Coquihalla River

Sowaqua River

Ten Mile Creek

Nine Mile Creek

MT. JARVIS

BEDDED RANGE

Railway Creek

5

To Hope

Peers Creek

THE COQUIHALLA

THE COQUIHALLA

Entering the Fraser just north of Hope, the Coquihalla has been a known gold producer for years, but the mining record for the river and its tributaries only begins about 1911. As in many other areas, activity has continued in a desultory way to the present, even though the Coquihalla River is awash in placer. It drains a slate belt that has a prominence of rich quartz from which most of the gold in the area originates. A great deal of gold has flowed down the Coquihalla Valley to settle well beyond the limit of this slate belt. You may also find platinum showing up in your pan.

The Coquihalla River ★

The more important work on the river was done near the mouth of Fifteen Mile Creek and the Sowaqua River, but good colours can be obtained at almost any point along the Coquihalla below Ladner Creek simply by overturning one of the larger boulders and panning the underlying sands. The bedrock here lies close to the surface, and the stream deposits have coughed up both coarse gold and platinum nuggets.

The recommended areas are where Ladner Creek enters the river, below the junction of the north and south forks, and scattered sites along the Coquihalla River between Ladner Creek and Peers Creek. Above Ladner Creek the river is mostly too rapid, and very few stream deposits remain. Below Ladner Creek, the riverbed widens, the grade is lower and mineral deposits begin to accumulate in the kinds of locations described on page 12.

You'll find just about any method suitable on this river: at various times we've used a gold pan, a dredge and a rocker to good effect, recovering everything from fine gold to nuggets and wire gold in quartz along its course.

Peers Creek ✶

This creek is well marked on the Coquihalla Highway, 18 kilometres (11 miles) east of Hope. The bars and banks linking the Coquihalla River where Peers Creek comes in are good places to start. A camp was established at Peers Creek's mouth in 1914, but it did not last long with the outbreak of war. When prospecting resumed at war's end, the benches and banks of the creek were again reported to be paying well. By 1932 gold had been retrieved from the streambed, banks and benches all the way to the headwaters. Peers Creek remains a solid prospect today. In the 1980s, while staking hardrock mineral claims for commercial interests around here, we dabbled on the side with a pan and portable dredge and got encouraging results with minimal efforts.

Ladner Creek ✶

From its headwaters in the mountains east of Hope, Ladner Creek flows southeast into the Coquihalla River. This creek has all the right features for placer accumulation, and up until the Second World War, mines known as the Pipestem, Idaho and Ladner claims operated upstream. You can still get to the old workings via Mines Road, which is well marked on the Coquihalla Highway.

Ladner Creek and its banks are lined with gold-bearing gravels. Chunks of white quartz with stringers have also been found here. In 1932 numerous small operations were reporting finds of coarse gold on both Ladner Creek and the Coquihalla River. The creek and its tributaries continued to be worked in later years, and placer miners made a decent living form pans and rockers. Today there are no commercial ventures on Ladner Creek; it is highly recommended for panning.

Fifteen Mile Creek ✶

Located about a kilometre north of Jessica Station on the old Coquihalla road, Fifteen Mile Creek is an intriguing site. Working by hand in the 1930s, miners recovered very coarse gold here, but the records suggest that at least 40 percent of the potential values escaped because of their primitive methods and tools. Later testing confirmed the creek's rich gold values, but the Great Depression and poor economy leading up to the Second World War put a stop to any serious exploration.

The old highway sprang into being when the railroad from Hope to Brookmere was abandoned and the track removed. Although obliterated in places, some sections of the old road are still accessible from Brookmere. Alternatively, the creek continues to beckon from its clear sign on the new highway.

BEAR NECESSITIES

We parked the pickup at a spot where they'd dug the gravel out to make the road a little wider, and we walked up an old trail to get to the creek on the other side. A branch creek came in there that we wanted to check out. We worked our way up to this creek, oh maybe a mile, starting out at about six o'clock in the morning, and came back on a different route—sort of making a big circle—returning at about four in the afternoon.

There was still a lot of leaves on the trees because it wasn't quite fall, and we'd stopped on a small hill looking down to where the pickup was when all of a sudden my partner said, "Look . . . LOOK!"

And just coming round the front of the pickup was a big, old sow grizzly. She had a cub with her that was about half her size—I'd say it was a year and a half old, anyway. She circled the pickup four times while we were watching, and on three occasions she stood up and sniffed the air. Now I always made it a point to never leave food out where bears or other animals could smell it, though we had lost our grub a couple of times anyhow. This day there was food in the box of the pickup, but there was a canopy on it, which was closed, and the food was in a box. And the wind was blowing from us down to her, so she couldn't smell us.

I had a rifle on my shoulder and so did the chap I was with, and I just went, "Shush . . . shush!" And the grizzly would stand up and she'd look and she'd sniff the air. When she got down she reminded me of a big pig because the hump on her back was rolling and her head was going from side to side, sniffing along the ground exactly where we had walked. She came up the old trail we'd taken in the morning and the cub was following right behind her.

We were only about 50 feet above her. She was walking right up that trail toward us and I whispered to he guy with me, "If she stops and stands up and looks, then I'm going to give it to her. But if she doesn't make any moves toward us, let her go and let the cub go, too."

I've never shot an animal in my life that I didn't have to shoot, but you don't want to take any chances with a grizzly and cub. But she just kept right on walking, following up the trail . . .

I didn't feel comfortable camping that night with her around, and we stayed out of that area the next day. Because the way I look at it, I'm in their territory as opposed to them being in mine . . . I'd advise people in the bush to always be on the lookout. You don't have to be paranoid about bears—just be aware. A female with cubs, even a black bear, is always dangerous and unpredictable.

One time when we were checking out some gold claims in the Fraser Canyon area and my son Bill was riding a trail bike, he came around a corner and nearly ran into two young cubs. One if them was an albino, you know, a white one. But it was definitely a black bear because Bill could see the mother close by. So he turned back, thinking he'd wait five minutes and she'd wander off with them into the bush. But she didn't. What she did was she put the cubs up a tree, then she turned around and now she was ready to fight! When Bill realized this, he just took off and he didn't go back in there the rest of the day.

—Jim Lewis

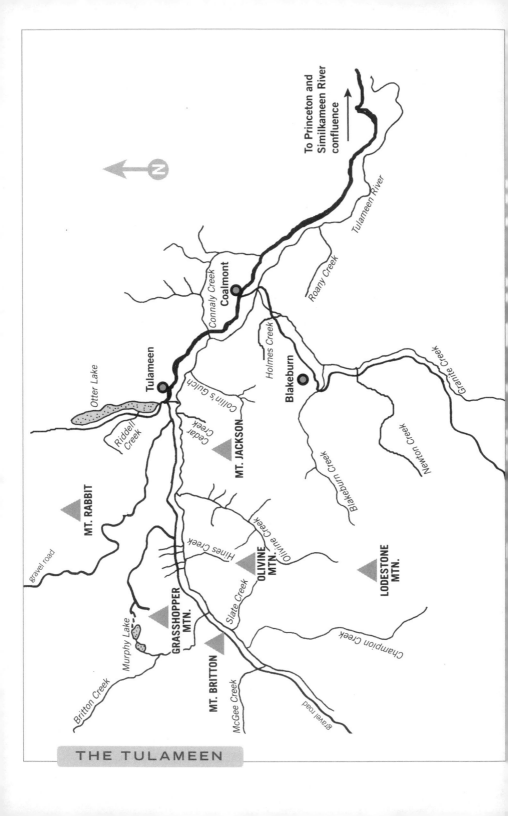

THE TULAMEEN

THE TULAMEEN

When John Chance discovered gold in Granite Creek near the village of Coalmont in 1885, placer interest in the Tulameen River soared. Some of the largest gold nuggets ever found in BC were later unearthed in the Tulameen watershed. A chunk found in 1887 brought a price of $900—more than $20,000 at today's gold prices! Around the same time, two nuggets retrieved from Bear Creek (now called McGee Creek—a Tulameen tributary upstream from the town) were valued at $400 and $450 each.

Aside from this weight of gold, the Tulameen is also renowned for its platinum and was the site of BC's first platinum discovery. The year was 1887. Granite Creek, which flows into the Tulameen River just below Coalmont, was again the site of discovery. Over the years, plenty of this precious white metal has been recovered from the Tulameen River and its banks.

The Tulameen River ★

The Tulameen has proved rich all the way from its confluence with the Similkameen River at Princeton upstream for 40 kilometres (25 miles), beyond Britton Creek. Close to the river's mouth the gold tends to be most coarse, but it retains a coarse texture all the way upstream. Platinum can turn up almost anywhere, and nuggets weighing 28 grams (1 ounce) or more have been found on occasion. Any black sand you find should be retained and assayed for its platinum values.

A bit heavier than gold, platinum is a silvery-white precious metal that is found in only four countries: the US, Russia, South Africa and Canada. Commercial demand for the metal arose only in the modern era thanks to its use in spacecraft, computers, automobiles, watches and jewellery.

Six kilometres (four miles) upstream from Princeton, Peterson Flat is formed by a widening of the Tulameen valley below a short canyon. Prospect diggings in the 1920s turned up good values here.

By 1908 Tulameen's placers had worked only in areas where the bedrock was close to the surface.

The year 1914 was good for the few people working the Tulameen River upstream from Tulameen. One miner earned more than $200 in two days. (With gold at $17.50 an ounce, that's more than 312 grams (11 ounces).

The next four locations are on the Tulameen River near where the respective creeks run in.

Roany Creek Vicinity ✶✶

The old Roany High Channel lies about six kilometres (four miles) downstream from Coalmont. The channel runs along the right bank of the Tulameen River opposite where Roany Creek comes in and about 30 metres (100 feet) above the river's present course. A gold-bearing gravel deposit lies toward the east end of this area, and both gold and platinum have been recovered there.

Britton Creek Vicinity ✶✶

In the years leading up to the First World War, a small company of miners made a living from a bar of the Tulameen River just above Britton (Eagle) Creek, working for three months each season during low water. They wing-dammed successive portions of the streambed and cleaned it down to bedrock. The company farmed this same bar year after year, profiting from the fresh supply of auriferous gravel washed down at high water each spring.

In 1926 a spectacular find was made about a kilometre below Britton Creek on the west side of the Tulameen. A pay streak was uncovered around and under a series of boulder dumps left by earlier placer diggings.

The Coalmont Hotel, circa 1955.

Here, 35 troy ounces of crude platinum were taken from short, narrow, open cuts dotted over an area of 60 metres (200 feet). The bench of this old channel is 90 to 100 metres (300 to 350 feet) wide and about 762 metres (2,500 feet) long. Practically no effort went into finding out the depth, width or extent of this pay streak, apparently because of the boulders. Since clearing away some loose boulders was a relatively small obstacle compared with the potential profits from bedrock gravels, it's difficult to understand why this area was not exploited. Because the river has changed course, the earlier bedrock here now appears to be about two metres (six feet) above the existing river.

Olivine and Hines Creeks Vicinity ✴

In 1947 a productive site was being worked 4 kilometres (2.5 miles) upstream from the village of Tulameen. Miners reported paying values from some low gravel benches on the right side of the Tulameen between Olivine and Hines Creeks. Look for a low bench 3 metres (10 feet) above the river and joined by a second bench rising gently to

. . . .

In 1965 a road was built
to allow prospectors to
work the south side of
the Tulameen River eight
kilometres (five miles)
west of Tulameen. The
point of so much interest
was a glacial outwash
deposit, part of a terrace
or bench high above the
river. Bench samples were
encouraging but never led
to any real exploration.

. . . .

In 1887 benches on
Granite Creek were
producing 9 to 28 grams
(a third of an ounce to an
ounce) per day for every
miner working a pan or
rocker. Engineers figured
that Granite Creek's gold-
bearing gravels extended
much farther than
originally supposed, most
likely running beyond the
creek's mouth through
a low sag (old channel)
in the mountains.

the north. Some old placer workings are still visible here.

Ancient Channel ✳

An ancient channel is indicated in the Tulameen's banks about a kilometre upstream from Hines Creek. A large body of gravel there at one time produced both gold and platinum.

Granite Creek ✳

With its headwaters in the Coquihalla Range (the Bedded Range on some maps), Granite Creek is just 40 kilometres (25 miles) long and joins the Tulameen River from the south, just downstream from Coalmont. Though this was the site of the first gold and platinum discoveries in the area, mining efforts have been confined by the creek's narrow, rock-walled canyons. The higher banks have been all but ignored, and the bars of this prolific gold and platinum creek offer excellent prospects.

Granite City ✳

A hundred years ago a city grew up on the left bank near Granite Creek's mouth. For a brief time, as many as 10,000 people thronged to Granite City, which is now a ghost town. A few skeletal buildings and a vandalized memorial are the only reminders of a time when the area thrived.

Of 40 leases held on Granite Creek in 1897, only 4 had any work done on them. The rest belonged to speculators who, rather than developing their properties, did only the minimum to maintain their lease rights.

In 1900 remnants of an old channel near Granite Creek's confluence with the Tulameen proved very rich in gold. The old channel appears to lie in the left bank of the creek, then crosses to the right bank upstream from Holmes Creek, likely continuing beyond a short canyon through which Granite Creek runs. Platinum and nuggets of gold weighing more than 14 grams (half an ounce) were recovered here in 1900. When bench claims in the area were prospected, the first shovel of material washed in a rocker produced a nugget valued at $23.40 (with gold at $17.50 an ounce).

Three kilometres (two miles) farther upstream, a pipeline was constructed in 1924 to bring water from Holmes Creek for a hydraulic mining operation on Granite Creek's banks.

A piece of land three kilomtres (two miles) above Granite City was the subject of a court action in 1900 when rock was displaced to lay a flume. Legal costs eventually forced the owner to sell.

In 1916 no placer mining was done on Granite Creek because extremely high water had washed out workings from the previous year.

Newton Creek Vicinity ★ ★

Although Granite Creek was generally thought to be worked out in 1915, new work below its confluence with Newton Creek soon changed people's minds. Lying just above a box canyon, this section had never

Bridge over the Tulameen River, 1885.

....

In 1960 work was suspended about a kilometre upstream from the mouth of Granite Creek when the compressor house and equipment were destroyed by fire.

....

A slide in 1900 destroyed sluice boxes and a flume on Slate Creek. Not to be discouraged, miners resumed their efforts, and in 1911 slate yielded a considerable amount of platinum and gold from shallow diggings.

been prospected before because a landslide had dammed the creek and formed a lake.

The new owners drove a tunnel through the slide area, drained the lake and sunk a shaft that hit bedrock at 4 metres (12 feet). They were rewarded with a striking quantity of coarse gold. A lot of gold and platinum has turned up around the junction of Newton and Granite Creeks, and along the benches downstream with Granite Creek there are indications of an old channel on Newton Creek, but only limited work has been recorded in the area.

Riddell Creek ✶✶

Riddell Creek used to join Otter Creek near its mouth but now flows into Otter

Granite Creek, 1880.

Lake (which formed after Otter Creek was dammed). The mountain to the west (Mount Riddell) is highly mineralized, so Riddell Creek will show white and silver platinum colours in every pan. For over a kilometre upstream, the creek has produced a lot of placer gold. Astonishing as it may seem, in the early years literally tens of thousands of grams of platinum were thrown back into the river along with black sand because miners of the day regarded the metal as worthless. It was a nuisance to operations because it was almost the same weight as gold and virtually impossible to separate with the primitive methods of the day.

Other Bright Spots

Collin's Gulch, Cedar Hines, Britton Slate, Champion and **McGee Creeks**, all tributaries of the Tulameen River, are also worth exploring. In recent years we've panned each one of these creeks and obtained gold.

Collin's Gulch

Upstream from Granite Creek, Collin's Gulch has shown promising values in the past but has never been mined. Heavy coarse gold has been found here.

Cedar Creek

Heavy coarse gold and platinum have also been found on Cedar Creek, which enters the south side of the Tulameen upriver, almost opposite Otter Creek.

Hines Creek

Eight kilometres (five miles) west of Tulameen on the south side of the river, Hines is a small creek that has produced coarse gold. Interest over the years has been minimal.

Britton Creek

Entering from the north three kilometres (two miles) west of Hines, Britton is another large creek that has never been the focus of any consistent mining effort. As at Hines, through, coarse gold has turned up along its course.

Slate Creek

About a kilometre upstream from Britton Creek on the Tulameen's south side, Slate Creek is another solid prospect with a history of coarse gold and platinum. Its name is omitted on most topographic maps, but it's the stream flowing in between Hines and Champion Creeks.

Champion Creek

Champion joins the Tulameen River from the southeast, about 11 kilometres (7 miles) upstream from Tulameen. This is a large stream with excellent prospects. The bedrock has never been worked.

McGee Creek

About a kilometre upstream from Champion on the north side of the Tulameen, McGee Creek (known in the early records as Bear Creek) flows over bedrock near its mouth. Big nuggets are a telling part of the history of the area. A nugget found here weighed in at $320 when gold was valued at $17 an ounce. In 1904 three miners working the mouth of Bear Creek recovered nuggets worth $120. Upstream the ground is deeper and has never been worked to any extent.

POT O' GOLD

One of the few times I was ever a little nervous was on the Fraser by Big Bar ferry. We had a couple of dredges here and were working away. There were high banks around us, and I looked up and though I saw a flash of something out of the corner of my eye. You know, something glinting in the sunlight, because the sun was bright that day.

So I look and all of a sudden I see this guy looking down on us from the top of the hill, and it's maybe, oh, a good half mile away from where we were working on he river and he's about 500 feet higher than us. I kept watching, just glancing every once in a while from under the hat I was wearing, and sure enough, I saw a rifle barrel.

And I thought, "Uh oh, uh oh, uh oh, uh oh."

So I warned the other guy that was with me. I shut my dredge off, walked over and told him, "Don't look at the moment and keep your back turned, but behind us there's somebody with either a rifle or binoculars, probably both, and I think they're watching us. I'm sure a saw a rifle barrel."

And he said, "What are we going to do about it?"

"Nothing," I said. "Not a damn thing. We're just going to stay right here . . . or maybe we better wander back to the trailer," 'cause we had rifles in the trailer. "This guy could be dangerous," I said, "or he might not be. I don't know what's going on here."

It was getting late in the afternoon and the sun was setting in the west—that's how I saw the glint of the rifle barrel I guess. "Let's just sit down here for a while and just have a coffee and relax and see what comes out of this," I said.

The water of the Fraser was too dirty to drink or cook with, and we had been getting ours from some other guys who had a trailer down a little ways from us—they had two wooden barrels for rainwater, which they were topping up from a spring somewhere. We were now down to about a gallon in our five-gallon jug, so I said to the guy with me, "I'm going to take a chance. You stay here just in case something happens. I'm going to take my pickup and drive up and see if I can get some water off whoever's up there."

There was a road leading up—it wasn't a very good road, full of switchbacks and boulders—but I got up there and came on a cabin step with the cabin built right back against the mountain behind them.

So I said to them, "Any possibility of getting some water?"

And the one guy said, "Sure. Help yourself. Fill your jug . . . Aren't you one of the miners that was working on the river today?"

Well, the only way he would have known that was from looking through binoculars at us because it was too far away to recognize our features from that distance.

And I said, "Yeah."

"Are you gettin' anything?"

"A little bit," I said. "Where's the water?"

He just pointed over there, like that, while they were sitting and smoking pot. So I don't say anything and I walk over with the jug. Well, I came to a hose end, but there was very little coming out of it and it was warm. And I thought, "There's gotta be better water than that here somewhere. This must only be overflow." So I walked maybe 50 feet up this little trail, and sure enough there was a nice, deep hole that I could sink the jug into and it held nice cold water. I'm filling the jug and I look up—just 20 feet away from me—and lo and behold there's all these marijuana plants growing. It was a marijuana plantation up there.

I walked back down and the guy says, "Oh, you filled your jug pretty fast." 'Cause if I'd have used the little hose that was just trickling I'd have been there half an hour. "I hope you didn't go up there too far," he said, "up that creek."

"No," I said. "I just went a little ways and I found water there and just dumped the five-gallon can in and that was it."

"You didn't see anything up there?"

And I said, "No. What was I supposed to see?" I knew bloody well what I wasn't supposed to see.

Then he said, "You wanna toke?"

"No, I don't use it," I said, "But you go ahead." And I got to talking to them a little bit and asked whether they spent their summers there.

"Yeah," he said. "We get outta' here in the wintertime. But we do a little mining and a little prospecting in the summer."

But I'm telling you, they were no more miners than I'm a farmer!

—Jim Lewis

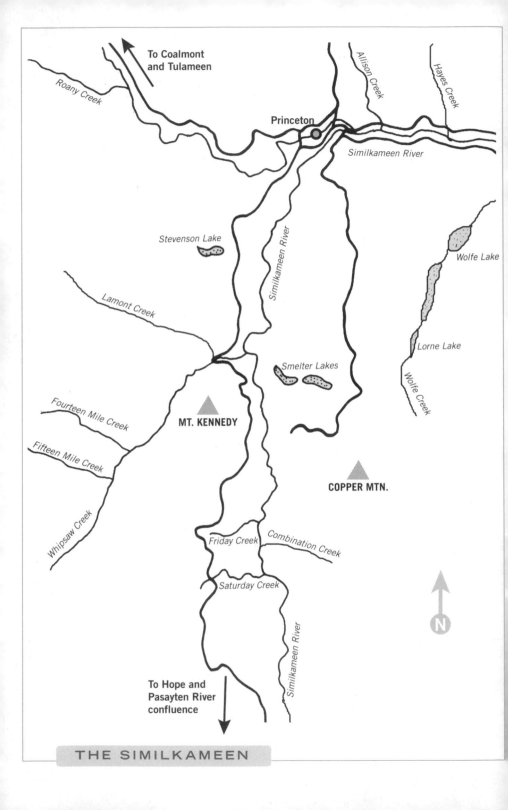

To Coalmont
and Tulameen

Roany Creek

Allison Creek

Hayes Creek

Princeton

Similkameen River

Stevenson Lake

Similkameen River

Wolfe Lake

Lamont Creek

Lorne Lake

Smelter Lakes

Wolfe Creek

Fourteen Mile Creek

MT. KENNEDY

Fifteen Mile Creek

COPPER MTN.

Whipsaw Creek

Friday Creek

Combination Creek

Saturday Creek

Similkameen River

N

To Hope and
Pasayten River
confluence

THE SIMILKAMEEN

SIMILKAMEEN COUNTRY

George B. McClellan made the first gold strike on the Similkameen River. The news spread quickly, and pacer operations were soon underway along the river's banks and bars. The interest was short lived. By 1860 most miners had traded in the Similkameen claims for Cariboo hopes as the gold rush swept them north.

The entire Similkameen River was known as the Roche River until 1925. The main branch was then renamed Similkameen, from the First Nations word meaning "red rocks." Both gold and platinum can be found along the banks of the Similkameen River, and most of the small streams flowing into it are also gold bearing. In spite of this, very little attention has ever been paid to them. The more serious prospecting has focused on the Similkameen itself, along the section upstream from its confluence with the Tulameen River at Princeton.

The Similkameen River ★
Gold can be panned from the banks, bars and benches, though some sections of the river are a bit forbidding. Good prospects abound in the area where Friday and Saturday Creeks flow into the main river south of Princeton. Here, gold-bearing gravels lie along both banks. Friday, Saturday and Sunday Creeks are all well marked on the Hope–Princeton Highway.

The Similkameen River winds its way near Princeton.

In 1897 a placer gold find on the Similkameen River resulted in a trail being built to open up access to the area.

Gold Crown ★

In 1889 assays were taken on a claim known as Gold Crown, located on the right bank of the Similkameen at its fork with the Pasayten River. Samples taken from a trench 2.7 metres (9 feet) wide, 3 metres (10 feet) deep and 7.6 metres (25 feet) long showed results as high as $450 to the ton. With gold at $16 an ounce, that's roughly 800 grams (28 ounces) of gold per ton. Poor access meant not much was ever done to take advantage of this spectacular find.

By 1900 some very rich pieces of wire gold had been found on the Similkameen River, but there was no equipment for mining. To make matters worse, a succession of high-water years kept destroying dams and ditches.

Whipsaw Creek ✶

Flowing into the Similkameen River south of Princeton, this gold-bearing creek should be worked in both its bed and its banks. Access is excellent from a logging road that runs alongside the creek (clearly marked on maps). In the early years, placer mining concentrated around the mouth and a short distance upstream.

Some productive benches are also located along this creek, and rich quartz ledges at

Whipsaw Creek bridge, 1957.

the headwaters no doubt contributed to the local placer deposits. The discovery of this quartz originally led to prospecting for hardrock claims. Placer exploration was never seriously undertaken on the creek itself or its tributaries.

Lamont Creek ✷✷

A good quantity of placer gold has travelled down Lamont (Nine Mile) Creek, which flows into Whipsaw Creek about a kilometre above its confluence with the Similkameen River. This creek is still a good panning location.

Hayes Creek ✷

Hayes (Five Mile) Creek, which follows the old Kettle Valley Railway form Bankeir and Jellicoe, flowing south into the Similkameen River six kilometres (four miles) east of Princeton is many kilometres long and drains a huge area. In places, fine gold lies in gravel close to the surface, and there are numerous benches along its course. Testing on Hayes Creek in 1933 turned up some comparatively coarse gold along with finer specimens. Platinum has also been found in this area. Like the other creeks mentioned, however, Hayes Creek was never worked to any extent. Be aware that much of the back road parallel to the creek borders private property.

Siwash Creek ✷✷ (This has the same name but it is not the same Siwash Creek mentioned in the chapter on Yale or in the Okanagan section.)

Flowing into Hayes Creek about 5 kilometres (3 miles) west of Jellicoe, this Siwash Creek drains an area 32 kilometres (20 miles) long and 10 kilometres (6 miles) wide. Down through the years, placer miners have retrieved plenty of comparatively rough-edged gold from the creek itself and from its benches. Miners at one time ran a hydraulic operation 11 kilometres (7 miles) upstream from the mouth, working on a productive bench 3 metres (10 feet) up on the west bank.

Several other benches border Siwash along its course, ranging from 3 to 15 metres (10 to 50 feet) above creek level. These appear to be old channel remnants that contain a considerable yardage of high-value gravels. Numerous test pits and open cuts dug to sample the ground between Teppe and Galena Creeks (and northward from there) all produced gold in testing operations.

. . . .

Vancouver Island's rivers, creeks and streams have their own bright spots, of a different colour altogether than the glimmering flecks of the Cariboo and the Fraser River. Six years into the Cariboo gold rush, the Vancouver Island Exploring Expedition was poking into the south Island's hidden treasures up the Sooke River, setting the foundations for what would become Leechtown. More about that later. There are other Island waters to whet the appetite. Notable finds were also cropping up along the San Juan River, Sombrio River, Jordan River, Cowichan River, Nanaimo River, along China, Mineral, Granite and Poole Creeks, the Franklin River and . . . wait for it . . . Gold River!

There are other good rivers, too, like Nitinat and Hewatches, but their history is relatively scant. Mentioning the major areas for the Island prospector and recreational panner doesn't mean they're the

Waiting at the CNR station in Leechtown, 1926.

The San Juan River near its mouth in Port San Juan, 1998.

only gold-bearing creeks. Far from it. Almost every creek and river on Vancouver Island will show at least two good colours to the pan. Mineral veins originally spawned by local volcanic activity are still being worked over by the West Coast's lashing winter rains and mountain snowmelt each spring. It's a different situation, geologically, than in the rest of BC, where northern glaciers swept down and retreated again, spreading their mineral bleedings as they went.

The high rainfall and heavy spring runoff are responsible for more than just renewing placer deposits. It's not unusual to be working riverbeds on Vancouver Island that have carved a course over 100 metres below the banks on each side. Spectacular to be sure, but this can present a challenge for the more casual panner. On the upside, there is an abundance of tricky locations that have never really been touched.

Haida Gwaii offers a different set of panning conditions that revolve around the gold-bearing sands of Graham Island. The island's black sands are far more extensive than any to be found on Vancouver Island. Early prospectors discovered that these sands extend all the

Gravel bar at the mouth of the Sooke River.

Klim Kwan First Nations village on Haida Gwaii, 1902.

way from Lawn Hill, about 13 kilometres (8 miles) north of Skidegate, up along the eastern shore to Graham Island's northern tip at Rose Point. The streams flowing out to sea across these beaches continue to concentrate the sands, which yield sparkling flecks of gold when worked by hand.

Although the origin of Graham Island's placer is not fully known, glacial drift from southeast Alaska—renowned for quartz veins with rich gold and platinum values—must have carried substantial deposits here. After a brief flurry of interest, placer activity was dormant for years. Interest was rekindled in the 1980s when individual prospectors once more began to sift through Graham Island's swirling beach sands.

SOUTHERN VANCOUVER ISLAND

The first gold strike on Vancouver Island came near the headwaters of the Sooke River in 1864. Explorers charting the river's course found gold deposits in the cracks and crevices of the river's bedrock. While there are no reliable statistics for the amount of placer recovered from Vancouver Island rivers over the years, the forces of erosion are such that at a rough calculation, $2 million in placer gold has washed down the Leech River alone. The major rivers that flow into Juan de Fuca Strait are all worth prospecting. As a point of interest, Juan de Fuca Trail runs along the Island's southern shore for 47 kilometres (29 miles) between China Beach and Port Renfrew. Pack a pan if you're hiking the trail—there are plenty of smaller creeks and streams to explore en route.

The first creeks featured in this chapter flow south into Juan de Fuca Strait and are west of Victoria.

The Sooke and Leech Rivers ★★

About 19 kilometres (12 miles) southwest of Victoria, the Sooke River empties into Sooke Harbour and Juan de Fuca Strait. The gold along the Sooke and Leech Rivers—a historic tributary 11 kilometres (7 miles) upstream—is derived from local quartz veins and stringers. Both rivers are well known for their productivity. Upstream locations can be accessed on foot via the Galloping Goose Trail, the old railway bed.

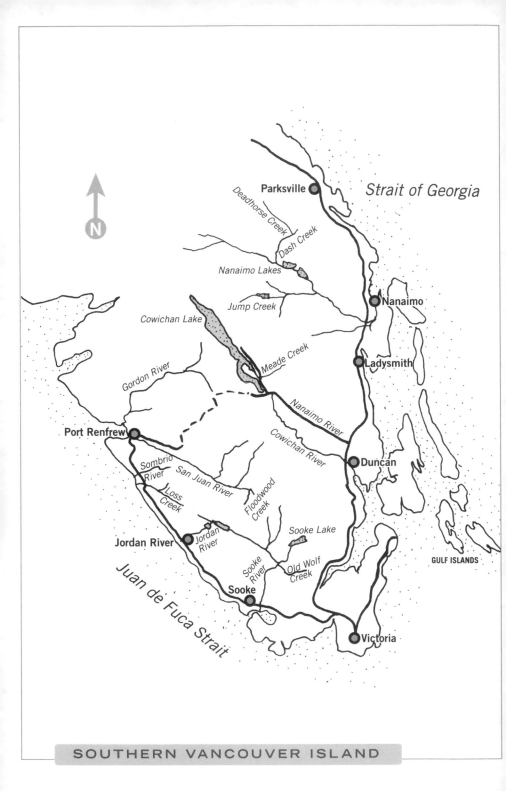

SOUTHERN VANCOUVER ISLAND

With gold valued at $16 an ounce, some $60,000 worth was recovered from the Leech River in 1895, 30 years after the first discovery was made. Without roads or machinery to assist them, the miners of the day reaped striking returns with only simple hand tools—shovels, sluices and their trusty gold pans.

In 1925 prospectors working the north fork of the Leech River discovered gold float from quartz veins in the bed and banks of the river. The flat at the confluence of the Leech and Sooke Rivers was later examined for the possibility of dredging, but nothing came of it. Several old shafts still exist in the area, the deepest running to about 10 metres (35 feet). Paying gravels have been worked all around here.

Leech Gravel Banks ✶ ✶

Gold has been recovered from gravel banks eight kilometres (five miles) up the Leech River as well. In 1931 during exploration of the high banks on the east side, bedrock was found 30 metres (100 feet) west of the present riverbed under some 12 metres (40 feet) of gravel that

Remains of the Leechtown government office, circa 1920s.

. . . .

A small company formed in 1901 to work three leases at the confluence of the Leech and Sooke Rivers. Though a successful enterprise, the company found its efforts (and profits) curtailed by high water and weak pumps.

. . . .

Leechtown and Leech River were named after Dubliner Peter John Leech, astronomer with the Vancouver Island Exploring Expedition.

overlay a bench. Prospectors traced this bedrock along a gradual slope for more than 60 metres (200 feet), to within 3 to 4 metres (10 to 12 feet) of the surface. There it turned and sloped down toward a hill, indicating the presence of an old channel.

Further work proved this old channel to be 2 metres (8 feet) deep, as much as 15 metres (50 feet) wide at ground level and narrowing to 3 metres (10 feet) wide at bedrock. An excavation into the old channel produced returns of fairly coarse gold.

Old Wolf Creek ✶ ✶

Another productive tributary of the Sooke River, Old Wolf Creek flows in nearly opposite Leech River. Gold was recovered here quite early on—in the late 1800s and early 1900s. The bedrock is the same formation as that of the Leech River, where quartz veins in the bedrock are responsible for some of the placer gold.

In 1933 two half-leases were staked on Old Wolf Creek a kilometre or so above Leechtown—now a name that endures only in the mining history of BC. The area explored lies 9 metres (30 feet) above the present creek, where an open cut shows bedrock to be dipping slightly into a hill, suggesting an old channel behind. Here miners found a depth of one to two metres (three to six feet) of gold-bearing gravel overlying bedrock. The gold was well worn and fairly coarse and ran at 890 fine, which is relatively pure for placer gold. Such striking results recommend the area for continued exploration.

Jordan River ★★

The Jordan River has coughed up more than a few treasures in the past. Approximately 50 kilometres (30 miles) long, the river flows into Juan de Fuca Strait 19 kilometres (12 miles) west of Sooke River and has plenty of promising placer holes. A logging road leads upstream, but the banks are steep in places, making them less accessible. The bed, banks and bars have proved to be worthwhile prospects all the way to the headwaters, which issue from a number of small lakes and swamps in the vicinity of Jordan Meadows.

Sombrio River ★

With extensive gold-bearing gravels recorded in this area, about 11 kilometres (7 miles) east of Port Renfrew, the Sombrio River continues to offer excellent prospects and is highly recommended. A signed gravel road leads down to Juan de Fuca Trail near the river's mouth. It's likely that the old channel of Loss River used to come out near here as well. These days the Loss River follows a new course to the east, where it has cut through the rim rock of its old channel.

Upstream from Sombrio River's delta, the terrain rises rapidly. At once time heavy gravel deposits filled the valley. Gold-bearing gravel is still widely dispersed here and extends three kilometres (two miles) upriver. The present-day stream has cut deeply through the gravel beds and deposited gold in the large delta area.

Near the beach, the banks at one time showed gravel ranging from about 30 to 90 metres (100 to 300 feet) deep, and the whole deposit was gullied by small surface creeks. By 1929 small test pits dug all over this gravel bar

Jordan River flume, 1913

First prospected in 1909, the Sombrio River produced gold from its bars, banks and riverbed. Limited hydraulic mining was later tried where the Sombrio and the Loss Rivers empty into Juan de Fuca Strait.

confirmed that the entire area was gold bearing. A mining plant was briefly considered, but the proponents lacked the funds to proceed.

San Juan River ✶

Farther west, gold has been found in nearly all the creeks and rivers leading into Port San Juan, especially the San Juan River. This is excellent country for a canoe or kayak expedition upstream. From the northwest, Browns, Wiggs and Coal Creeks flow into the Gordon River, which forms a broad estuary with the San Juan River and enters Port San Juan at the far end of the bay from Port Renfrew. Be sure to pan any black sand you find—fine gold has been found in the black sand of the delta area. Good values have been recovered along the San Juan River Valley, about a kilometre and a half upstream from the river's mouth.

Driftwood covers the beach at Port San Juan with Port Renfrew in the distance.

Floodwood Creek ✶✶

In 1983 nuggets weighing more than 14 grams (half an ounce) were discovered from gold-bearing ledges along Floodwood Creek, which flows into the upper San Juan River. Located northwest of Jordan Meadows, this creek is remote but accessible by logging road.

The remainder of the creeks in the chapter flow east into the Strait of Georgia, north of Victoria.

Cowichan River ✶

Known as gold bearing by the late 1800s, the Cowichan River has never been worked in any methodical way. Gold has been found in the banks, bars and streambed from the river's mouth to its source in the Vancouver Island Range, above Cowichan Lake—the auriferous belt of Vancouver Island. The river's gold is derived largely from the erosion of quartz veins along its course, and most of the streams flowing from the north into Cowichan Lake are worth panning.

Meade Creek ★

An excellent area to pan for gold, Meade Creek flows southwest into Cowichan Lake three kilometres (two miles) west of the town of Lake Cowichan. Start panning about a kilometre above the railway bridge and work your way upstream another kilometre to where the creek flows through a canyon area. Within the canyon, fine gold has been retrieved from material scraped off the bedrock as well as from the sands around the roots of trees near the high-water mark. Upstream beyond the canyon, gold has been panned from a nearby overburden on bedrock that lies 6 metres (20 feet) above the high-water mark. Though fine, as many as 40 colours have been taken from one pan in this area.

Nanaimo River ★

The north and south forks of the Nanaimo River carry gold in their bars, banks and beds. Despite all its promise though, the Nanaimo River has never been the site of serious placer mining. Because coal

Looking over falls on the Nanaimo River, 1870s.

mining and logging were local industry staples from the late 1800s through to the mid-1900s, placer and other mining exploration was extremely limited. Roads now allow relatively easy access to this area, but logging operations are active during weekdays so proceed carefully.

In 1935 placer mining training camps were set up along the Nanaimo River—an indication of its bright prospects for panning.

Jump Creek ✶ ✶

A recent foray along Jump Creek, which flows into the south fork of the Nanaimo River from Jump Lake, turned up some sparkling returns.

Deadhorse Creek ✶ ✶

Accessible by a logging road that turns up Dash Creek, Deadhorse Creek contains fine gold. About eight kilometres (five miles) upstream from the junction with Dash Creek, a vein about 10 centimetres (4 inches) wide is exposed in the right side of the Deadhorse Creek bed. This vein is the source of the placer that flows down the creek. Be careful: there are a couple of old mining shafts in the area. An old mining tunnel is located just below a set of falls, and some of the same gold vein is exposed inside the tunnel. The tunnel was stable during recent exploration, but caution is advised whenever you explore old mine workings.

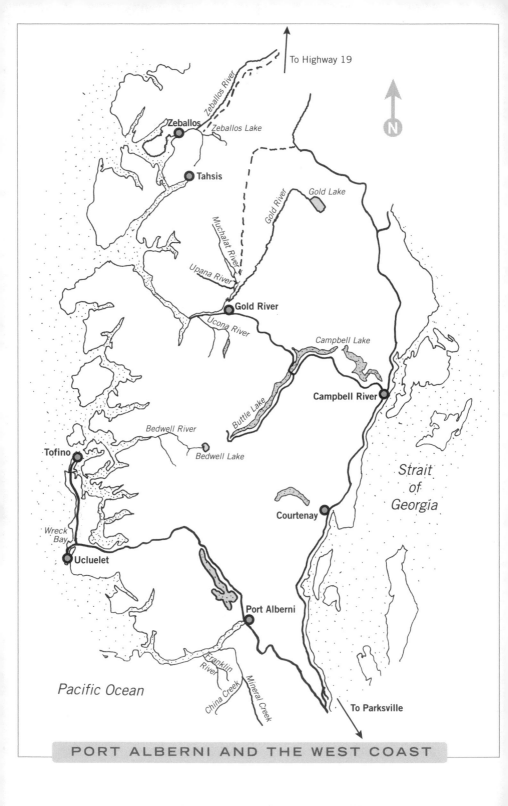

To Highway 19

Zeballos River

Zeballos

Zeballos Lake

Tahsis

Gold Lake

Gold River

Muchalat River

Upana River

Gold River

Ucona River

Campbell Lake

Butte Lake

Campbell River

Bedwell River

Tofino

Bedwell Lake

Strait of Georgia

Courtenay

Wreck Bay

Ucluelet

Port Alberni

Pacific Ocean

Franklin River

China Creek

Mineral Creek

To Parksville

N

PORT ALBERNI AND THE WEST COAST

PORT ALBERNI
AND THE WEST COAST

Much of the remaining placer history on Vancouver Island is concentrated in the creeks on the south side of Alberni Inlet, particularly China Creek and its tributaries. Several other major river systems of the Island's west coast—including the Bedwell, Gold and Zeballos Rivers—are also proven gold-bearing watersheds. The Bedwell River is inaccessible by road. The best access is by boat through Clayoquot Sound from Tofino. To access the Gold and Zeballos Rivers, drive north to Campbell River, then follow the signs from there. Farther north, rich seams of copper and coal fuelled hardrock mining interests, overshadowing placer activity.

China Creek ★

China Creek flows into Alberni Inlet about six kilometres (four miles) south of Port Alberni. The road to Bamfield parallels the creek for several kilometres and crosses it about a kilometre upstream from its mouth; a separate logging road leads upstream for some distance. China Creek has a long-standing reputation as a placer creek and has been prospected from its mouth upstream for at least 19 kilometres (12 miles).

Large gold veins at the creek's headwaters are the most likely source of China Creek's colour. The veins run mainly in sandstone, which is easily eroded by winter freezing and thawing. The 1893 mining records say the Chinese had already been working the area for 30 years with

Exploring China Creek, 1880s.

pans and rockers, recovering plenty of placer gold. Because it is a fine, floury texture, however, much of the potential values undoubtedly escaped during the cleaning process. Rockers are almost useless for recovering fine gold.

The benches along China Creek will yield many colours to the pan. We've also found quite a number of small pieces of gold adhering to quartz rock, pieces that looked as if they had travelled only a short distance. Minerals found in the Shaw Creek and Cous Creek areas (on the opposite side of the Alberni Canal from China Creek) prove the gold range extends across the inlet in that direction.

Mineral Creek ✷✷

The upstream logging road along China Creek crosses Mineral Creek, a tributary that's well worth exploring. Very coarse gold has been found here, both on the surface and slightly below the surface a short distance upstream from the mouth. The placer gold in China Creek displays two distinct colours: the pale gold comes from Mineral Creek, while the darker gold—worn and smoother—originates farther upstream on China Creek. Gold-bearing gravel lies in the benches on both sides of Mineral Creek. Small pits dug by prospectors over the years have been remarkably free of boulders, which makes the ground that much easier to work with a pan.

Early Chinese workings can still be located on Mineral Creek. Rocks were piled in mounds so they would not have to be moved again while working the ground, a classic Chinese technique.

Granite Creek ✶✶ (This has the same name but it is not the same Granite Creek mentioned on page 98.)

A smaller creek still farther upstream on China Creek, Granite Creek (this local name is not marked on topographic maps) has turned up coarse gold from cracks and crevices. The creek is swift, running over large boulders, and panning around these rocks at one time paid well. The benches and banks also produce good colours.

Franklin River ✶

A little over three kilometres (two miles) past China Creek, the Bamfield road crosses the Franklin River. In 1893 miners panning gravel from any of the creeks feeding into the Franklin River were recovering placer gold. The gravel was being worked only on the surface—no digging was done at this time. Pool Creek is a gold-bearing tributary of Corrigan Creek, which flows into the

A series of companies staked leases on Wreck Bay, but their legal rights soon reverted to the Crown when a succession of hard seasons left them unable to fulfil their requirements or make the necessary assessment payments.

In 1888 Chinese miners fled the Bedwell River area after the death of a worker raised fear and superstition in the camp.

Gold has been found on both Amos and Gold Creeks, located near Cape Scott in the Quatsino Mining Division at the northern tip of Vancouver Island.

Franklin River a few kilometres upstream. The Bamfield road crosses both these creeks another 4 to 5 kilometres (2.5 to 3 miles) farther on from the Franklin River crossing.

Wreck Bay ✶

Located near Ucluelet at the south end of Pacific Rim National Park Reserve, Wreck Bay (Florencia Bay) was a significant placer beach at the turn of the century. The Gold Mine Trail into the bay commemorates this mining past. Fine gold was found in and around Lost Shoe Creek in the yellow beach sand, as well as in the black sand that runs along the bay's entire length. Mining activity was first recorded in the area in 1901, and nearly $10,000 in gold was recovered when prices were at $17 an ounce—that's roughly 16 kilograms (558 ounces) of placer.

Interest in the area never panned out into any serious exploration due to the wet conditions and high water table on the Pacific coast. Today, national park restrictions apply: you can explore, but natural resources are strictly protected and cannot be removed from the park.

Bedwell River ✶✶

From the river's headwaters at Bedwell Lake in Strathcona Provincial Park, the Bedwell River flows through pristine wilderness on its course to Clayoquot Sound. The river is remote, with no roads or settlement along its length, and although flow is moderate during the dry months, it is subject to rapid flooding during winter, which no doubt enhances its historic placer deposits.

Three kilometres (two miles) upstream from the river's mouth, Ursus Creek flows into the Bedwell, and there are plenty of bars to prospect upstream and downstream from the forks. The river flows through a wide valley, and you can canoe or kayak upstream for some distance, although four sections of rapids require portages.

Gold-bearing quartz veins are visible along its course, and a considerable amount of gold has been recovered from the bars, banks and streambed. In 1898 a group of experienced miners staked numerous claims along the river, which was then known as Bear River. Gold has also been found around the headwaters, which now lie within Strathcona Park boundaries in the Vancouver Island Range of mountains.

Gold River ✱

From its headwaters in the Vancouver Island Range at Gold Lake, Gold River drains a large, mountainous area and is joined by several large rivers and numerous smaller creeks on its way to Muchalat Inlet. North of the town of Gold River, the main branches are the Upana River and Muchalat River, which flow in from the west from lakes bearing their names. At the town itself, the Heber River, De Loriol Creek and Ward Creek flow in, while downstream toward the inlet, Flash Creek, Cascade Creek, Deer Creek, Ahaminqas Creek and the Uconoa River all empty into Gold River.

As its name suggests, gold has been found almost everywhere along these watercourses, and the whole area is worth exploring. A main road leads through the town downstream to the inlet, where a pulp mill was located. Logging roads provide good access to the upstream rivers and creeks.

Zeballos River ✷✷

The biggest rush on Vancouver Island drew thousands of eager prospectors to Zeballos in 1935. Nearly 8,500 kilograms (300,000 ounces) of gold were mined between 1936 and 1943, with 400 men working in 30 mines. The mine remains are mainly on the east side of the Zeballos River.

When this river was first examined for placer in the early 1900s, several discoveries were made just upstream from the river's mouth in Zeballos Inlet. Since then, a number of profitable ventures have worked their way up the Zeballos River and along its north arm, which is now bordered by a logging road. Like many of the Island's other rivers, gold has been recovered from the bars, the banks and the streambed. It's an excellent area to pan.

Gold veins and stringers occur in the whole area, and some of the veins are rich in gold. Any of the numerous creeks and streams that flow into the Zeballos River are also worth exploring, bearing, as they do, names suggestive of their gold history: Blacksand, Pandora, Golden Gate, Hidden Valley and Goldvalley Creeks to name a few.

Exploring China Creek, 1880s.

Privateer gold miners with gold bricks, Zeballos, 1938.

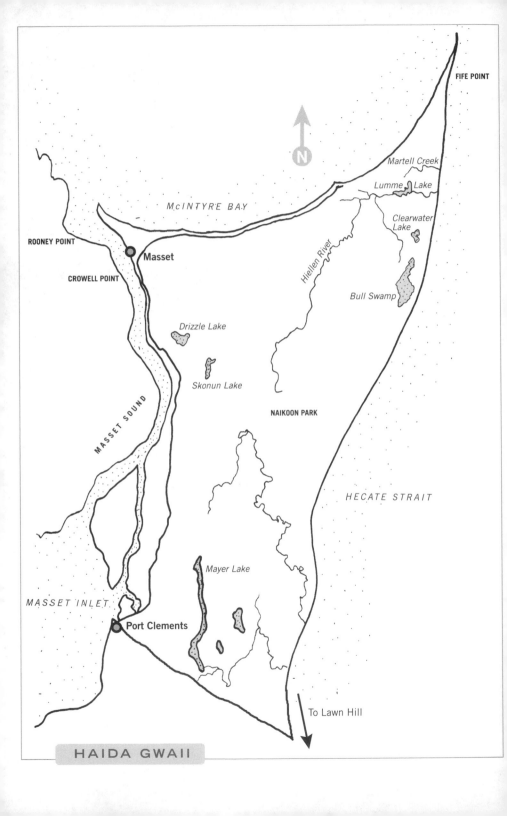

FIFE POINT

Martell Creek

Lumme Lake

Clearwater Lake

McINTYRE BAY

ROONEY POINT

Hiellen River

CROWELL POINT

Masset

Bull Swamp

Drizzle Lake

Skonun Lake

NAIKOON PARK

MASSET SOUND

HECATE STRAIT

Mayer Lake

MASSET INLET

Port Clements

To Lawn Hill

HAIDA GWAII

HAIDA GWAII

Accessed by ferry from Prince Rupert (on the BC mainland), Haida Gwaii (formerly known as the Queen Charlotte Islands) offers a unique, natural environment for outdoor adventure. The largest islands in the archipelago are Moreseby Island and Graham Island, the latter being the prominent location of placer deposits. These are concentrated mostly in the black sands along the eastern shore north of Lawn Hill, an area now largely encompassed by Naikoon Provinical Park.

Rose Point ★

On the northeastern tip of Graham Island, gold and platinum have been recovered from the black beach sand to the east and west of Rose Point (also known as Rose Spit). The beaches on both sides of the spit are extensive and productive.

Martell Creek ★

Located six kilometres (four miles) south of Fife Point, gold-bearing sands accumulate at the mouth of this small stream where it cuts through the high bank of the beach. Cinolla Mines once operated in this vicinity. The upper layers of sand near Martell Creek are heavily concentrated and contain approximately 50 percent black sands. These have been reported to yield as much as 14 grams (half an ounce) of placer gold per cubic yard panned. The depth of the sand ranges from a couple of centimetres to about two metres.

Prospecting was going on in 1930 at Masset Sound, but lack of machinery all but stopped work. By 1935 several individuals were working the black sand deposits in this area and making a profit.

In the area known as Lawn Hill on the eastern shore, prospectors have discovered paying quantities of gold.

Bull Swamp ✶✶

Likely the best area to pan on Graham Island, Bull Swamp starts three kilometres (two miles) south of Clearwater Lake (near Fife Point) and extends six kilometres (four miles) farther south. The creeks around this area concentrate the sands and provide a natural sluicing action. Numerous specks and pieces of fine gold can readily be seen, and much of the yellow sand here also contains gold values

Masset Vicinity ✶

Another large deposit of black sand is located about a kilometre south of Masset on Masset Sound between Rooney and Crowell Points. Test pits dug into a bank 4 to 6 metres (15 to 20 feet) above the high-tide line on the west side at one time revealed layers of black sand up to 30 centimetres (12 inches) thick at depths of 2 to 3 metres (6 to 9 feet). Away from the water's edge, prospectors worked the sands as far as 15 metres (50 feet) back into the trees and recovered up to 28 grams (1 ounce) of gold and 57 grams (2 ounces) of platinum to the ton.

About a kilometre south of Crowell Point, a small stream flows in from the west and has concentrated these black sands. In 1928 miners were making very good wages here, shovelling into sluice boxes and

Totems at Skidegate, 1890.

pumping water from the stream. Colours panned anywhere in this area show a fair weight and size—by no means is this fine or flour gold. This area, more than 24 kilometres (15 miles) southwest of Martell Creek, illustrates the wide distribution of gold values.

TIT FOR TAT

One time in winter, between Hope and Princeton, I was about seven miles off the highway. It was all straight uphill and I mean steep, too. You had to have a four-wheel drive to get in. I had a brand new truck and these two geologists were with me—geological engineers, actually—and they were both well into their 60s. One was about 68, 69, and the other was 64 or 65.

We parked on the side of a valley, walked across and stayed inside a mine tunnel because that was the warmest place. It was avalanche country and the buildings were condemned because of avalanche hazards. So we stayed right in the underground tunnel, in one of those crosscuts—a little tunnel that goes off to the side—and that was fantastic. We collected maybe 500 or 600 pounds of samples, and by the third evening, about six o'clock, we were finished.

"Well," I said, "you guys want to spend the night here?"

And the older guy answered, "Not if I can help it."

"Okay, I'll go out and get the pickup."

I didn't feel like hand-packing the samples 600 yards across to where the truck was, so I said I'd try and drive it up there—even though it was an old road that had washed out at the creek. It had also snowed about seven or eight inches during the three days we were there. Anyway, I walked across and I jumped into the pickup, turned the key on . . . Absolutely nothing!

I thought, "What? I can't have a dead battery!" So I tried it four or five more times.

It was a standard shift and I even put the clutch in and everything else, you know, trying to get the thing to start. Finally I got out, opened the hood, and I'm looking . . . No battery!

The cables weren't cut. They undid them. Took the battery. Well!

Remember, I'm seven miles off the highway here. So I crossed back over to the tunnels and I said, "Look, I've got to walk out or something. Someone's stolen the battery. You guys stay here and I'll be back."

I didn't want them to walk out with me. They were older, and I didn't want any heart attacks or anything like that on my hands. Anyway, I walked out and going down was just fine. Easy. And when I got on the Hope–Princeton Highway I just put my arms up and stopped the guy coming—like: I need help! I got a ride into Hope and the only place that was open was the Husky Station. By now it's about 10 o'clock at night. I bought a battery and asked the guy if he could take me back out there. He didn't have a four-wheel drive so I knew he'd never get up the hill but he said he'd give me a battery strap and take me as far as he could.

Well, he got about half a mile off the highway and now he's spinning and sliding, and there's steep drop-offs there. And I said, "Hold it, hold it, hold it! You're going to go over the bank first thing you know, and then we'll really have a problem. Let's forget it."

So I paid him for his trouble and I took the battery. Alternately, I had it on one shoulder, then on the other one. I had it in one hand, I had it in the other hand, then two hands, and I'm trying to keep the battery acid off my clothes if I can.

Well I slipped and I slid and I packed it about six and a half miles up the mountain. But the time I got back it was a little after seven in the morning and I'd been going all night. So I put the battery in and of course, right away—Boom!—she fired up immediately. No problem! I put her in gear and I went across that creek like it was on fire cause I didn't care anymore I was so angry! I really didn't care!

When I got over there I got them up and put the samples aboard. They had coffee going then, so I had a cup of coffee with them and then we took off. We got into Merritt—it's now 10 o'clock in the morning—and these geologists have their vehicle there, so we loaded up the samples into it and they left.

Now I'm still so bloody angry that I don't want to go home and I don't know what to do with myself. The hotel was open at 10 o'clock—the beer parlour—and I walked in what used to be the ladies' side. There was a wall there and at one time it used to divide what was the ladies' side and the men's side from one another. So I'm sitting there, and all of a sudden I hear some guys come in on the other side. And I say to the bartender, "Draw two." Glasses of beer in those days I think were 20 cents or something. And I'm sitting there, still burnt about this battery, when I hear from the other side, "How did that Cornbinder start this morning?"

And the guy said, "Oh, perfect, perfect."

"Oh, you bought a new battery?"

"Oh, shit no!" He said. "I found a four-by-four in the bush and I took the battery out of it and now I got a brand new battery in my truck."

Well I swear that the hair just stood up on the back of my neck! I walked out the door I come in and was about to get into my pickup when I thought, "No, no, no—I'm going to find out who these clowns are."

Although I'd left my beer on the table, I walked back in the other door—the same door they'd come in—and I'm sitting there now and there's three of them—two of them sitting together and one sitting at another table right next to them, and they're yakking back and forth and I'm looking at them.

And I thought, "Ahh, by Jesus! What should I do about this?"

Well, the bartender looked at me and at the table I had just vacated with a glass and a half of beer on it, and I said, "Draw two."

Well he looked at me funny and I said, "Just draw two will you!"

I drank one of those beers and I got up. I noticed now that they each had three or four beers in front of them and I said to myself, "Well, I think it must be getting-my-battery-back time." I walked out, went around the corner, and saw this International there. Cornbinder's an old slang term for an International. This was kind of a high panel one they used to have years ago, but with windows in it. Travelall or whatever they called them. Anyway, I saw it sitting there at the curb, and I said, "Oh yeah, that's fine."

Well I always kept a set of bolt cutters with me, usually 30-inch bolt cutters, so I turned around and walked back to my pickup, pulled the bolt cutters from behind the seat, placed them next to me and drove around the corner, and parked right in front of this International. I just opened the hood—they all opened from the outside on those days, there was no such thing as a latch inside—and I just opened the hood and I took the bolt cutters and I went SNIP, SNIP to the two battery cables and I took the battery, put it in the box of the pickup, and I drove away. I just left them right there with no battery and I thought, well, tit for tat.

But when I thought about it later on, I got even more angry. Because if someone had got hurt or had cut himself really badly, somebody could've died over that episode. It's not very damn smart to go and pull a trick like that in the bush.

—Jim Lewis

PART III

THE FRASER, THOMPSON AND COLUMBIA RIVER SYSTEMS

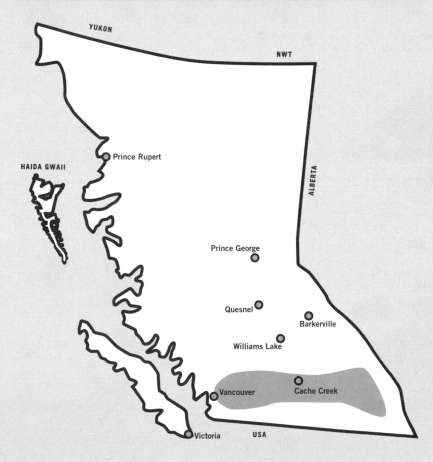

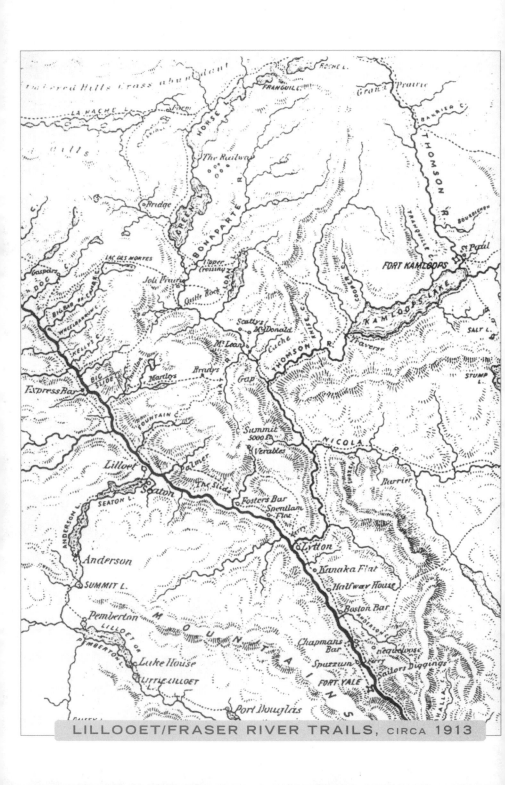

LILLOOET/FRASER RIVER TRAILS, CIRCA 1913

. . . .

The fabulous Fraser Canyon has always been, and remains even now, a very scenic area. The Fraser River, which flows through this canyon, is fed by thousands of tributaries that together drain more areas of BC than any other river system. Many of these tributaries contain gold-bearing gravels, so the Fraser is known to carry gold along its entire length. The late Dr. George Dawson of the Geological Survey of Canada, who travelled from Ottawa in the 1880s to explore, map and survey in BC and other provinces, and whose published reports of his exploration of this area are relied on for accurate information even today, once called the river "a giant sluice box."

With constant "sluicing" occurring through natural erosion, bringing fresh gold-bearing materials into the Fraser River drainage area every year, gold can still be recovered in good quantities by panning along the river. The gold itself is a fine, flour type, as it has been carried many kilometres by the churning waters of the Fraser before settling on bars and low bank areas. During low-water periods, many of these bars can be worked with good success.

Miner with rocker box set up to rework old tailings, circa 1930.

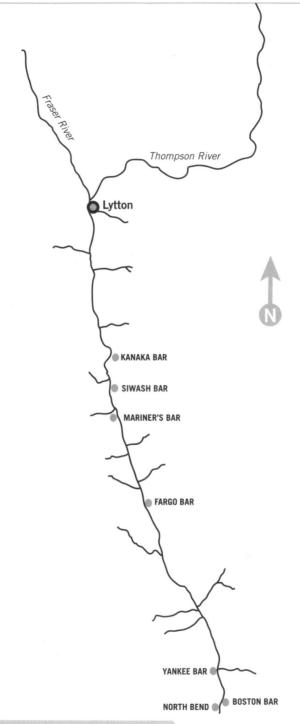

Fraser River

Thompson River

Lytton

KANAKA BAR

SIWASH BAR

MARINER'S BAR

FARGO BAR

YANKEE BAR

NORTH BEND   BOSTON BAR

FRASER RIVER BARS

LYTTON AREA

Boston Bar ✶

Boston Bar was first reported on in 1875, when placer miners using gold pans and rocker boxes on the banks and bars of the Fraser River met with success. In 1885, reports say, when gold was valued at approximately $16 per fine ounce, hand panning these banks and bars recovered some $20,000. In 1893 miners constructed dredges at Boston Bar, intending to work the river-bed. These large dredges, similar to those used in the Yukon, were not successful in the Fraser because of the fast current and large boulders encountered; after numerous accidents, miners abandoned efforts to remove the gold-bearing gravel from the bed of the river by this method.

At North Bend, across the Fraser River from Boston Bar, leases were acquired to placer mine the banks and bars of the Fraser River. People worked both sides of the river with good success.

In 1896 the Wendell Company and the Ottawa Mining and Milling Company, whose property was located 2 kilometres (1.5 miles) west of North Bend on the banks of Fraser, used monitors (water under pressure) to wash the gravel into sluices. They were successful until the creeks supplying the water dried up. Scarcity of water and the need for repairs to the flume line kept actual mining to a minimum; in fact, it came to a stop every year.

Gold dredger at Boston Bar, 1897.

From 1881 to 1895, the Fraser River from Lytton to Yale reported a yield (documented by gold buyers) of $1,070,850—with the price of gold at that time being a mere $16 per fine ounce!

The Agnes Hydraulic Mining Company also worked the banks of the Fraser at North Bend. Approximately a kilometre below Keefers (Keefers's location is marked on topographical maps), there is a bench adjoining the railway tracks where coarse gold in paying quantities has been found. This spot was considered one of the good locations on the Fraser.

Limited placer mining continued between Boston Bar, North Bend and Lytton on the banks and bars. By 1900 the yield of gold from this area was $28,017.69 at $16 per ounce. High water in the river reduced the yield that year, though the bars produced well.

For years the bars and banks of the Boston Bar/North Bend area have been worked at low water in the early spring and late fall, and they continue to produce gold to this day.

Kanaka Bar ✶✶

Located approximately 12 kilometres (7.5 miles) below Lytton as the river flows, between Boston Bar and Lytton, Kanaka Bar has produced a considerable quantity of gold, yet it has never been mined to any great degree. The pay streak is found from the surface down to false bedrock on the east side of the Fraser River and is in a readily accessible area. On the opposite bank, the west side of the Fraser, prospecting was done at the river's edge and on the low benches. Rich ground was found on the west bank close to the Kanaka Station of the Canadian Pacific Railway.

At Kanaka Bar there is the possibility that an old channel exists on the river's west side behind a large rock promontory. To the north, the drainage waters flow north; the ground flattens gradually here and is covered with light gravels. On the north end of this area the possibilities are far more attractive, as concentrations of gold may have occurred under the flat ground. Practically no exploration work has been carried on in this area, so it is a good prospect.

Lytton ✶

Lytton, a quaint town located where the Thompson and Fraser Rivers converge, has a mining history dating back to 1874. Businesses in the town purchased gold from miners for many years. Records show that in 1885 over $15,000 of gold (at $16 per ounce) was purchased here.

The Van Winkle Hydraulic Gold Mining Company held a lease on the west bank of the Fraser three kilometres (two miles) above Lytton. This company held benches rising 34 to 121 metres (110 to 397 feet) above the high-water mark, and coarse gold was found in the gravel. Gold totalling $3,800 (1894 prices) was obtained by sluicing. In 1895 a poor water supply resulted in little mining, though $2,168 worth of gold was recovered.

It is reported that in 1900 a bucket dredge was built and tried at Lytton. It worked well. Gravel dredged from the Fraser at Van Winkle Bar produced good results; however, following a disagreement between the owners, the bucket dredge was tied up and not used. By 1903 it had sunk and had to be refloated and rebuilt. It was again used successfully, but because of the low water level, it could not be moved upriver. But during the time it worked, it produced excellent results.

Another dredge was constructed at Lytton around 1900. By 1904 it had become apparent that this new dredge had been improperly built because the machinery—not strong enough to withstand the heavy strain—kept breaking, so it was eventually dismantled. The last recorded dredging operation near Lytton ended when the original dredge was wrecked by high water.

This area of the Fraser is still an excellent spot to pan for gold. We have personally panned along these banks and bars between Lytton and Lillooet and obtained satisfying results.

Group at the shaft house at Van Winkle, 1898.

WILD THINGS

I guess a prospector's worst nightmare is to run into a wolverine—or more than one. Only once in my life did I run into wolverines, and there were three of them. I was in a remote area of BC, and since they're nearly an endangered species, I'm not going to say where it was. However, I was up at about 6,500 feet elevation, in the summertime, travelling along in the trees, and I came to a small dip, like a miniature valley. I was standing there for a few minutes, just looking down at the countryside and debating whether I should keep going forward or turn toward the left and head on a small but recognizable trail.

As I was standing there, not moving, I looked down and all of a sudden these three little furry animals came into view. They smelled a bit like skunks, were about 14 inches high and possibly 2.5 to 3 feet long—and they were playing! Two would play and one would watch—they were in the bright sunshine—and all of a sudden the third one would join in and one of the two that had been playing would be on the alert. I watched them for about five or six minutes and it was amazing the way they were playing among themselves and just seeming to enjoy themselves, like three young puppies. I don't believe they were very old; I think they were from one litter, or maybe it was the mother and two offspring. However, they were all approximately the same size.

When I realized what they were, having read about them in the past but never having seen one in real life, I thought, "Oh-oh, oh-oh—get outta here and don't let them spot you, because you might have a problem." They've been known to bedevil prospectors and trappers and anyone or anything else that comes in their path, especially if you get in their territory. They've been called every name in the book, from scroungers, gluttons, Indian devils and skunk bears to a few that don't stand repeating, and they have a uniformly evil reputation. They're not often confronted in the bush, but I've been told by reliable people that even a bear or a cougar will back off if a wolverine is in the area. They're real carrion eaters and if they do go after a kill—they'll drive a bear or cougar off.

—Jim Lewis

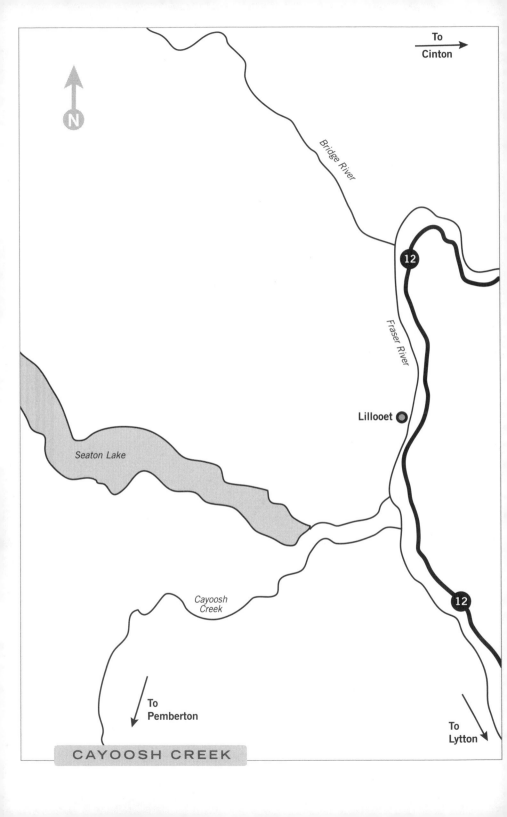

To
Cinton

N

Bridge River

12

Fraser River

Lillooet

Seaton Lake

Cayoosh
Creek

12

To
Pemberton

To
Lytton

CAYOOSH CREEK

LILLOOET AND AREA

Lillooet ★

It is possible to pan all the bars and gravel benches along the full distance of the Fraser River above Lytton and up toward the town of Lillooet, with a good chance of recovering gold colours or fine gold. Do not overlook the banks themselves—during high water, gold is deposited around boulders and in all areas where the water slows down; this is happening each and every year as gold travels downstream from the many creeks, gulches and tributaries that make up the Fraser River system.

There are many streams in the area right around the town of Lillooet that are gold bearing.

The yield from the area was quoted at $63,915 (1881 prices), and by 1884 had increased to $107,934. In 1886-87 it was recorded that the gold from Cayoosh Creek was the most valuable (coarser and with less quartz than other areas, and also of greater fineness), so the claims were the richest in the district.

Cayoosh Creek ★

Leaving Lillooet and heading on the road to Pemberton, you will come to Cayoosh Creek. This is one of the best gold-bearing creeks in the area. The gold is very coarse, and the creek's banks are an excellent place to explore. Gold in nugget form has been recovered upstream and downstream from the point where the highway bridge crosses Cayoosh Creek.

It is incredible that this creek, within four hours' walk from the town of Lillooet, was passed by thousands of experienced miners for more than a quarter-century, yet its riches were not discovered until the late 1800s. Chinese miners, many of whom returned to China in 1887, principally mined the claims—all by hand. The majority of these claims were located on the first 16 kilometres (10 miles) of Cayoosh Creek, starting a short distance above the confluence of Cayoosh Creek and Seton Lake Creek, and then upstream in a south-southwesterly direction to a point where Cayoosh Creek is intersected by quartz-free gold-bearing ledges. These ledges were discovered in September 1886, but no mining has been done above them. The ledge crossing Cayoosh Creek was subject to violent upheaval in the past, and fragments of it are found far away.

Note that during spring runoff and after heavy rains, the creek runs very fast and should be treated with caution.

Cayoosh Creek, circa 1910.

Bridge River ★

The Bridge River contains gold in the gravel along its banks and bars from its confluence with the Fraser River, between six and eight kilometres (four and five miles) north of Lillooet, up to the dam that now forms Carpenter Lake. Years ago this area was worked by the Chinese, and even today their workings are still visible.

McGillivray Creek ★★

McGillivray Creek has long been known as a good placer location. Gold is found in quartz veins along this creek's length, which is approximately 47 to 48 kilometres (29 to 30 miles). The headwaters are on the height of land that separates McGillivray Creek from the headwaters of Cadwallader Creek, which is the creek that flows northward past the abandoned Pioneer Mine and the mining town of Bralorne and then into the Hurley River between Bralorne and Gold Bridge. McGillivray Creek runs into Anderson Lake.

To get to McGillivray Creek, take Bridge River Road, which leads from Lillooet to Gold Bridge and Bralorne. From Bridge River Road, take the road that runs across the top of Mission Dam toward Shalath. From Shalath take Seton Highline Road through Seton Portage. McGillivray Creek is roughly 14 kilometres (9 miles) beyond Seton Portage.

The high cost of piping and the limited access in the early 1920s meant that no mining of any consequence was ever done here, and it is still a good creek in which to locate placer gold. The best areas are the gravel banks on both sides, which are a considerable distance in length. Approximately one kilometre above the creek's confluence with Anderson Lake, an old river channel was located and a gravel face about 9 metres (30 feet) high and 2 metres (7 feet) long was opened up. A small amount of mining was done with excellent results. This area is good for panning.

BRALORNE AREA

Cadwallader Creek ★

This famous gold-bearing creek has been known since 1886. Many hardrock gold properties and some active hardrock mines such as Bralorne Mines and Pioneer Mine were developed along its length, and gold was being obtained as early as 1891. Cadwallader Creek should not be overlooked, as it still produces gold from its banks and bars.

Tyaughton Creek ★

This creek is located beyond the town of Lillooet on the Lillooet–Bralorne road. The area is excellent for recreation and camping. Tyaughton Creek has been worked in the past. About 21 kilometres (13 miles) up Tyaughton Creek from Carpenter Lake there are extensive benches of gravel on both sides of the creek, which contain gold in paying quantities. We have personally panned and used a suction dredge in the area with good results.

Marshall Creek ★

Formerly called Alexander Creek, Marshall Creek is also in the Bralorne area and empties into Carpenter Lake. You can reach it by taking the Lillooet–Bralorne road (clearly indicated by signs) and watching for the creek sign beside the road. If you get to the road to Tyaughton Creek, you've gone too far. Large banks and benches of gravel on Marshall

Lorne-Pioneer Mine at Cadwallader Creek, 1898.

Creek have produced gold in paying quantities, so this is an excellent creek to pan or dredge.

Eldorado Creek ✶✶

This creek is a tributary of Gun Creek and is approximately 13 kilometres (8 miles) long. It is gold bearing for its full length, with the gold distributed equally from the surface downward to the bedrock. This is an excellent area to prospect, but it is located at a high elevation, so the summer months are the only feasible time to check it.

CLINTON

In any area where Chinese miners worked, you will find rocks and boulders piled neatly in rows— sometimes as far as 30 metres (100 feet) away from the site. Because they had no equipment of any kind, the miners did this so they would not have to move the rocks over and over again. Miners who did not follow this custom had to work around their boulders and rock piles.

Watson Bar Creek ★ ★

To get to Watson Bar Creek, take the Bridge River Road from Lillooet toward Bralorne. Approximately 180 metres (600 feet) after you cross the Bridge River (the first bridge on this road), you will see the Slok Creek Forest Service Road on the right. Take this road, and you will cross Watson Bar Creek via a bridge. The north and south forks of this creek are both gold-bearing streams. On the north fork, an old channel exists at the upper end of the creek. This channel is visible about a metre above the creek bottom. In the lower reaches of the creek, gold is found in the top 45 centimetres (18 inches) of ground above a badly fracture diorite bedrock channel, which averages 5.5 metres (18 feet) in width. About 4 metres (12 feet) of low-grade gold-bearing gravel covers this channel. Once you remove this gravel, you will find gold here that is coarse and rough edged. This area has yielded 57 grams (2 ounces) per linear foot along its length.

Crows Bar ✶✶

Situated on the Fraser River about 80 kilometres (50 miles) above Lillooet, this bar has long produced gold in paying quantities. It can be reached by road from Jesmond, skirting Big Bar Mountain and dropping down the river valley. Crows Bar is clearly indicated on topographical maps. Old workings were carried by the Chinese miners on both sides of the Fraser River about 30 metres (100 feet) above the low-water mark.

A wide bench extends on the east side of the Fraser at a height of about 45 metres (150 feet) above the river, sloping down toward the river on the downstream side. A second bench about 30 metres (100 feet) high continues around the bend of the river beyond this point. The general opinion held by mining people is that an old channel passed under this bench area, joining the present channel of the Fraser River about half a kilometre downstream. The old workings seem to have been confined to the section of the old channel exposed on the face of the bench, and none of these workings were carried back any great distance or height above the river. A bed with a width of about 4 metres (12 feet), made up of what appears to be old river gravels, has been exposed here. Recoveries made from the old riverbed have been more than usually good, and the character of the gold is quite distinct form the rest of the bench material, being considerably coarser—up to split-pea size—whereas the fold found in the Fraser River is unusually fine flour-type gold.

Fenton Creek ✶✶

In 1932 a new find was made on this creek, which branches off Churn Creek near its headwaters. The headwaters are located on Poison Mountain, which lies about 90 kilometres (56 miles) due west of Clinton, at an elevation of some 2,000 metres (7,000 feet). Coarse, rough-edged gold was found in the creek gravels, which vary in depth from 1.5 to 9 metres (5 to 30 feet) deep. At one time, because of the short season, this area was not worked much and only narrow trails were made; there are now roads leading in. Fenton Creek is found on topographical maps. To get to Fenton Creek, take the Cariboo Highway (Number 97) and turn left on the road leading to Empire Valley/Gang Ranch. Cross the bridge over the Fraser River and follow the road leading to Black Dome Mountain.

Fairless and Borin Creeks ★ ★

Both of these creeks have had paying quantities of gold. They are located about 80 kilometres (50 miles) as the crow files, but about 169 kilometres (105 miles) by road, northwest of Clinton at the 1,200 to 1,500 metre (4,000- to 5,000-foot) level of Black Dome Mountain. To reach these roads, take the Cariboo Highway, then turn off onto the Empire Valley Road and follow it to a point 16 kilometres (10 miles) past Churn Creek Bridge, where you turn onto a mining road and continue 24 kilometres (15 miles) to the creek area.

Big Creek ★ ★

Big Creek flows into the Chilcotin River a few kilometres below Hanceville (reached by road from Williams Lake). Gold was first discovered in this creek in 1910, when gold and platinum values were found. Big Creek drains a large area and received only limited prospecting; the small amount of prospecting done did not locate bedrock. The discovery on the creek was made about six kilometres (four miles) north of the Big Creek post office. The area is about a kilometre (half a mile) wide and five kilometres (three miles) long, situated between two canyons where the creek has cut its way through the rock. This area is north and east of Lillooet and the Bralorne area, and it is in the gold belt leading into the Cariboo gold-bearing regions (Wells, Barkerville, Likely, Horsefly).

Other Bright Spots

The following three creeks should not be overlooked today. The modern creeks have cut the old channels (much like in the Cariboo area), so gold-paying gravel is not confined to the creeks. The higher banks could be good possibilities.

Old-time miners used short sluice boxes that allowed quantities of gold to escape over the end, so a lot of gold was lost and not recovered.

Churn Creek ✶✶

This creek has its headwaters in the Poison Mountain area and is a known placer creek, providing good returns to miners. Coarse gold can found near its headwaters. There are strong indications of old channels on Rock Creek (now known as West Churn creek), where good pay has been found on bedrock.

Poison Mountain Creek ✶✶

This creek has also produced gold in paying quantities. It is located near the headwaters of Churn Creek. The placer gold in Poison Mountain Creek occurs at and in the bedrock cracks of the present narrow streambed. At places along the creek, remnants of an older and slightly higher narrow channel have revealed gold values. The glacial debris in this area contains gold that is considered to be local in origin, with an average size ranging from a pinhead to a grain of wheat. Very little fine or flour gold is recovered. The gold is also rough edged, with the occasional piece being flattened and well worn and apparently not far from its original sources in the rocks of the area. The colour is a characteristically dark bronze/gold shade, and only small amounts of black sand are recovered with the gold.

This creek was first identified as being gold bearing in 1932 and has never been mined out. It is therefore a good creek to prospect.

Lone Cabin Creek ✶✶

This creek has its headwaters on Red Mountain, located in the area of Poison Mountain, and has been known to contain gold in its gravel. Lone Cabin Creek flows into the Fraser River above Big Bar Ferry.

. . . .

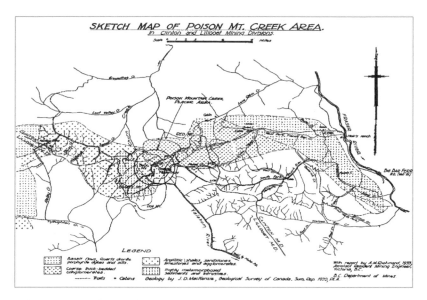

This sketch map (circa 1933) of the Poison Mt. Creek area is taken from Jim
Lewis's extensive mining library and is typical of those submitted by mining
engineers in the early 1900s.

In the late 1800s, after the Fraser River and Cariboo excitement in the
placer-mining field had slowed down, prospectors started to examine the
Thompson River from Lytton upstream into the Kamloops and Nicola
Valley areas. Gold was first discovered in the area by First Nations in
the 1850s and sold to Chief Trader McLean at Fort Kamloops. Gold
was also discovered on the Nicomen River near its junction with the
Thompson in the late 1850s.

The Thompson River is large and fast flowing; however, it has many
bars that contain gold, as do its banks. It is stated that, in 1903, people
were recovering gold at Lytton and upstream by hand with pans and
were shovelling the gravel into sluices and rockers with no machinery

other than manual labour. The amount recovered was $39,600. Bearing in mind that gold was valued in the area at approximately $18 an ounce, this yield would have been approximately 62,000 grams (2,200 ounces).

The best times to pan for gold along the Thompson River from Spences Bridge to the Ashcroft area are early spring and fall. On the Thompson River, areas worked by hand year after year produce gold in paying quantities, as every year the high water brings down fresh deposits of gold. These fresh deposits are far below the surface and are easily panned.

Spences Bridge, Cook's ferry, where gold was first found in the Thompson River.

THOMPSON RIVER

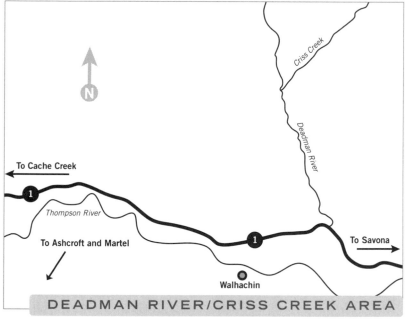

DEADMAN RIVER/CRISS CREEK AREA

Martel ★

Gold has been found by panning a small creek situated 3 kilometres (2 miles) northwest of Martel, a station on the Canadian National Railway line adjacent to the highway and approximately 13 kilometres (8 miles) from Spences Bridge on the Spences Bridge–Cache Creek highway. Quartz veins from several centimetres to 1.8 metres (6 feet) in width outcrop in this area, and these veins are the source of the gold-bearing gravels and gold found in the creek, which flows into the Thompson River. Roads from the highway lead into this area.

You may have to cross private land to gain access, so be sure to request directions and permission. People in the area are informative and helpful.

Ashcroft ✶ ✶

Gold was located in good quantities east of the town of Ashcroft on the northwest side of the Thompson River, about a kilometre from the Cache Creek–Kamloops highway.

The Canadian National Railway passes through this area. Test pits have been dug across the old river channel, which now forms a high bar about 240 metres (800 feet) wide and a kilometre and a half long, adjoin the northwest bank of the Thompson on the inside of a long bend of the river.

Consistent values amounting to approximately 14 grams (half an ounce) of gold and platinum per yard of gravel were found from the

Chinese prospector crossing Ashcroft Bridge, 1882.

surface to a false bedrock of blue clay. About 25 percent of the total value of gold and platinum received consisted of platinum. The miners worked the area mainly by hand, using sluices and rockers.

During low-water periods in the spring and fall, the benches in the river are accessible, and good paying quantities of gold and platinum can be recovered. You may have to cross private property to gain access; if so, be sure to obtain permission.

Criss Creek ★ ★ ★

This creek, located in the Ashcroft mining area, was discovered to contain gold in the gravels in 1916. Several leases were taken up from the mouth upstream for some kilometres. This area was prospected with good results; however, due to the First World War, no actual mining was carried out. (Gold was not considered an essential mineral during the war years.)

Criss Creek flows into the Deadman River, which is located near Savona on the Cache Creek–Kamloops highway. At the junction of Criss Creek and the Deadman River, gold has been recovered in good quantities. A road parallels Deadman River to the junction of Criss Creek. Reaching areas of Criss Creek farther upstream involves some strenuous hiking. However, the creek remains a good area to pan.

The Thompson River, like the Fraser, is considered a giant sluice box because of the many gold-bearing streams depositing their materials in the river.

Deadman River was the location of a placer mining camp set up by the provincial government during the Depression for the purpose of teaching people how to use a gold pan and rocker.

Deadman River ✶

Mining was done by hand on the Thompson River just below its junction with Deadman River, approximately 1.5 kilometres (1 mile) below the outlet of Kamloops Lake. On the banks of the Deadman River, about a half a kilometre upstream, one-metre deep test pits panned out good quantities of fine gold. The Deadman River is a small stream and, with the exception of a canyon about 180 metres (600 feet) long about 2 kilometres (1.5 miles) upstream, is easily accessible. No old workings are present, suggesting that this is virgin ground and an excellent area to pan. As much of this area is First Nations land, you must first obtain permission to gain access to the creek.

NICOLA RIVER AREA

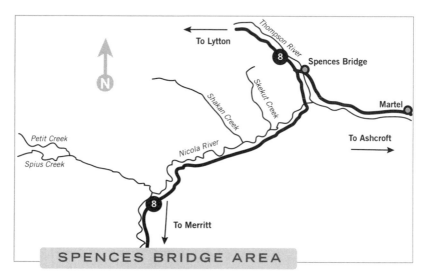

Highway 8 follows the Nicola River all the way to the town of Merritt. Access to the river is excellent, and there are also many pull-off spots close to it where recreational vehicles and tents can be used. All along the length of the Nicola River the bars and banks are great areas for panning, as is the riverbed itself.

Skekut Creek ★★

Skekut Creek is located approximately 16 kilometres (10 miles) from Spences Bridge on the highway to Merritt. This creek flows into the Nicola River from the west side and drains a large area. Gold has

Approximately five kilometres (three miles) from Spences Bridge on the highway to Merritt, gold has been recovered from the banks of the Nicola River.

been found near its headwaters. Once again, much of the land here is privately owned, and permission for access must be sought from the owners.

Shakan Creek ✶

Gold has been found in Shakan Creek, which is located approximately 23 kilometres (14 miles) from Spences Bridge in the direction of the town of Merritt. This creek also flows into the west side of the Nicola River. First Nations own this land, so obtain permission to cross their property to gain access to the creek.

Spius or Petit Creek ✶

Spius or Petit Creek is a large stream entering the Nicola River approximately 50 kilometres (30 miles) from Spences Bridge and 16 kilometres (10 miles) from Merritt. This stream drains a large area and is known to be gold bearing, having veins outcropping in the drainage area. Placer gold has been recovered from both the mouth of the creek at its confluence with the Nicola and upstream. Platinum has been recovered along with the gold. No serious placer mining has been carried out here. The valley at the mouth of the creek is approximately a kilometre wide, so there are large gravel beds.

KAMLOOPS AREA

Tranquille River ★

This river was found to be gold bearing and was prospected at the beginning of the 20th century. About 4 kilometres (2.5 miles) upstream from the mouth of the river, on the left bank, there is a bench that was prospected with good results. At the junction of the north and south forks of the Tranquille, about 9 to 12 metres (30 to 40 feet) above the river, lies another bench where good prospects were found. This location is evidently an old channel that was once occupied by the present stream. A considerable section of this old channel probably still exists. It may have escaped the scrutiny of the miners who worked in the vicinity in the early days because they concentrated mostly on the creek itself and did not examine the high banks. The river bottom and low banks at or near the high-water mark have also been worked for many years and have yielded gold each and every year due to erosion and spring runoff. The gold is coarse and washed smooth by water action.

Panning and rockers were the only systems used during these early times. Dredging was tried on the Tranquille River in the early 1900s, but as was usual with bucket-type dredges, most of the gold recovered was not saved, in part because of the fineness of the gold.

Little placer mining has occurred since the Second World War, and the gold remains in the Tranquille River. This is an excellent area to pan and prospect; in fact, the BC Tourism Branch in the City of Kamloops actively encourages panning here.

North Thompson River ★

Approximately 18 kilometres (11 miles) north of Kamloops on the North Thompson River, the river, bars and benches produced good results before Jamieson Creek enters the river. Gold is also found on the banks (west side) of the North Thompson as far back as the foothills, a distance of about a kilometre. This seems to indicate the gold has been derived from the range of hills on the west side of the river.

About 19 kilometre (12 miles) north of Kamloops at Edwards Point, the gravel is gold bearing far above the low-water mark. The gold has been deposited by high water and has undoubtedly come from Jamieson Creek, and each year more gold is brought down by the runoff. About a kilometre above Edwards Point, where the North Thompson is fed by Jamieson Creek, the ground has been tested and found to give good results. Approximately eight kilometres (five miles) farther upstream on the North Thompson, where it is fed by Skull Creek and other creeks, good gold-bearing gravel has been found. Above Skull Creek is a canyon, and this area is also gold bearing.

Good surface prospects were found on the North Thompson River between Louis Creek and Barriere Creek. Payable bars and gravel banks are numerous all the way up to the Clearwater River.

Jamieson Creek ★

Approximately 19 kilometres (12 miles) north of Kamloops, Jamieson Creek empties into the west side of the North Thompson River. About a kilometre upstream from the mouth of the creek, ledges containing gold were discovered. These ledges account for a portion of the source of gold.

Around 1.5 to 2 kilometres (1 to 1.5 miles) upstream from the mouth of Jamieson Creek, benches on the side of the creek have been tested and have yielded good results. The results were also excellent when the creek bottom and bars were tested.

Gold has been found in the banks and bars about eight kilometres (five miles) upstream from the mouth of the creek. There are many veins containing gold in this drainage area. The higher banks and areas where bedrock is exposed have also yielded good results.

Louis Creek ✷

Louis Creek enters the North Thompson River above Skull Creek. It has been known for many years that there is gold in Louis Creek, and small-scale work—by hand—has taken place. High values of platinum as well as gold were found from the mouth and farther up the creek. Upstream, where the creek emerges from a narrow valley, is a good stretch of gold-bearing gravels. Some gold concentration has resulted from the water movement around the rim of a wide-sweeping area of the creek where it joins the North Thompson. The North Thompson is gold bearing here, too, and coarse gold has been recovered.

In 1896 lack of equipment and low water were factors that hampered placer mining; the same conditions, plus the resulting lack of finances, also restricted work in 1897.

In the 1950s, copper mining was the trend. In many of the copper mines, gold was recovered as a by-product, and in some instances paid a good amount toward the cost of mining. Placer mining was largely ignored.

There are veins in the rock on both sides of Jamieson Creek with assays as high as 218 grams (7.7 ounces) to the ton. There is no doubt that these veins deposit gold into Jamieson Creek each and every year.

Historically, Louis Creek was being prospected in the early 1920s at its confluence with the North Thompson, and excellent results were obtained. Later, in 1927, the lower reaches of Louis Creek were prospected and panned with good results. Miners considered building flumes in order to hydraulic-mine the area with monitors, using gravity water pressure, but in 1930 the miners working the area disagreed on the methods of the work being proposed and a legal argument ensued. Due to this and other difficulties, the company involved went broke and not much was accomplished. A new company was formed later and did some work with good results. However, lack of finances hampered its efforts, and by 1931 several of the leases had been dropped and the company's affairs wound up. By 1933 the Great Depression had taken its toll here, too. From the creek's mouth to approximately five kilometres (three miles) upstream, various individual miners continued to work Louis Creek using hand methods such as pans, sluice boxes, rockers or shovelling the gravel by hand, and they made a good living.

Lanes Creek (formerly known as Noble Creek) ✷✷

Lanes Creek, as well as Dixon Creek, flows into Sargent Creek before joining the Barriere River a short distance north and east of the town of Barriere on the North Thompson. The creekbed and banks as well as the benches of Lanes Creek were prospected and good results found. Hardly any mining was done here during or after the war years. Much of the land in this area is privately owned. Request permission before crossing or using private areas.

Dixon Creek ✷✷

In 1900 Dixon Creek was examined with a view to using large bucket dredges, the same type used in the Yukon. However, because of the fineness of the gold and the small size of most of the creeks, dredges couldn't be used.

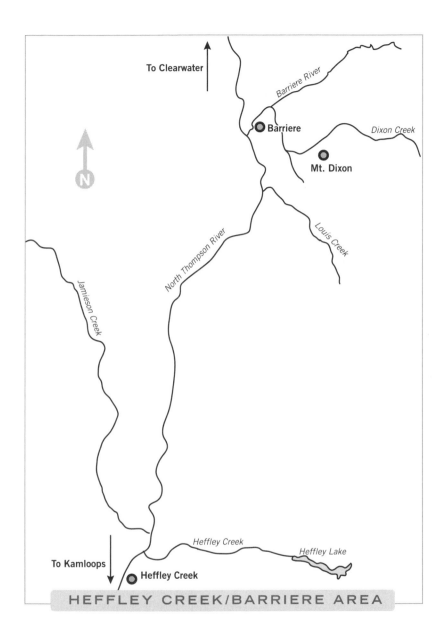

To Clearwater

Barriere River

Barriere

Dixon Creek

Mt. Dixon

Louis Creek

North Thompson River

Jamieson Creek

Heffley Creek

Heffley Lake

To Kamloops

Heffley Creek

Large areas of Dixon Creek's benches and bars have revealed gold. The gold recovered was coarse; small nuggets have been found under and around the boulders in the creekbed.

Barriere River ✶✶

Lack of financing during the Depression put an end to all mining operations, and even after the end of the Second World War little placer mining on any large scale was carried on.

This river has been known to contain gold since at least the beginning of the 20th century and possibly before that time. The veins that outcrop along the river's drainage system are probably the source for this gold. The feeder creeks along this watercourse have also undoubtedly enriched the riverbed, banks and bars.

Eakin Creek ✶

This creek flows into Lemieux creek just north of the town of Little Fort on the North Thompson River. For several years prospectors held placer claims on Eakin Creek from its junction with Lemieux Creek upstream. The creek was staked in 1922 for about 1.5 to 2 kilometres (1 to 1.5 miles) upstream from its mouth. The low flat near the mouth of this creek is well worth panning. The benches in the first two kilometres along the creek contain gold in the gravel. There is also a low bench in this area that is an excellent location to pan. Considerable coarse gold was found on Eakin Creek, so prospecting here has produced very satisfactory results.

In 1925 prospectors were doing handwork on both Lemieux and Eakin Creeks and on most of the tributaries flowing into both of them from the west. Some attempts were made to sluice ground in

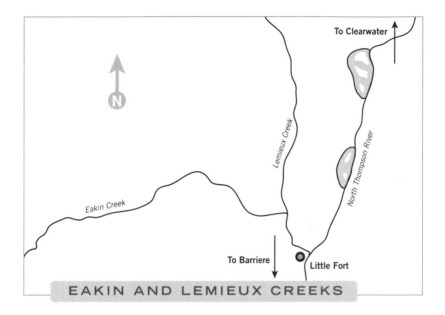

To Clearwater

Lemieux Creek

North Thompson River

Eakin Creek

To Barriere

Little Fort

EAKIN AND LEMIEUX CREEKS

both creeks and from the bench areas in both creek valleys. Below these benches are extensive gold-bearing flats. There are many areas of both Lemieux and Eakin Creeks where it is possible to pan several colours of gold to every pan. A lot of the land around here is private, so be sure to request permission to access it.

In 1930 gold nuggets were found above a conglomerate formation that Eakin Creek cuts through. Coarse nuggets were found in the section of the creek valley where boulder-strewn flats extend away from the creek for a distance of approximately one kilometre, over widths of 15 to 45 metres (50 to 150 feet). Some people tried mining by hand, but the boulders hampered the sluicing operation, and there was no machinery available at that time to move boulders. In 1931 the necessary machinery was installed, some ground sluicing was attempted in the bed of Eakin Creek and good results were obtained. The gold in this area is quite coarse, and good-sized nuggets were recovered here.

Heffley Lake ✶

This area, approximately 32 kilometres (20 miles) northeast of Kamloops and easily accessed by road, has long been known to have gold in all of the tributaries flowing into the lake from the south. All of the creeks cut through large stratas of glacial gravel, known as moraines. It is possible that the glacial moraine has covered an old channel. The present creek beds consist of a stratum of blue clay. Wherever miners have broken through this blue clay, fairly coarse gold—both lemon-coloured and rusty in appearance—has been found in a bed of gravel.

This area was prospected in 1932, and today would be an excellent area to pan and recover gold. Do not ignore the bars and banks in any of the creeks, as these can be very good. Old channel remnants above the creeks can also be rewarding to pan.

Clearwater River ✶

The town of Clearwater is the gateway to magnificent Wells Gray Provincial Park. The staff at the Information Centre provides knowledgeable and excellent service to tourists visiting the area. Please note that there is no panning in provincial parks without permission.

The headwaters of the Clearwater River are approximately 16 kilometres (10 miles) from Quesnel Lake. Many gold-bearing streams

In 1900 gold and platinum were assayed from the Clearwater River. The results were: gold—454 grams (16 ounces) to the ton; platinum —3,515 grams (124 ounces) to the ton.

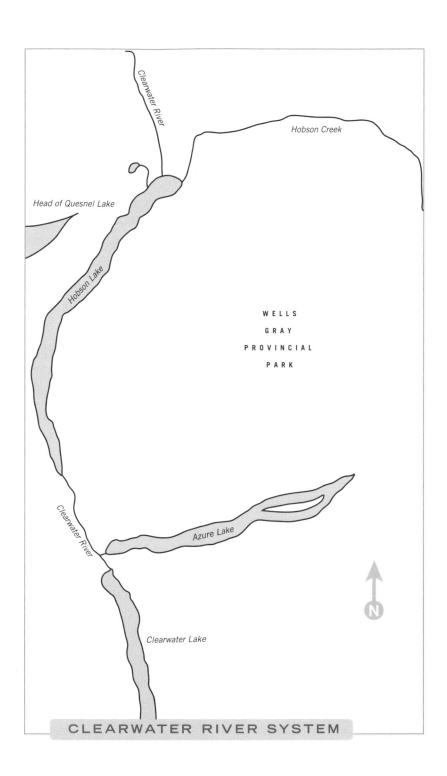

Clearwater River

Hobson Creek

Head of Quesnel Lake

Hobson Lake

WELLS
GRAY
PROVINCIAL
PARK

Clearwater River

Azure Lake

Clearwater Lake

N

CLEARWATER RIVER SYSTEM

The name was changed from Hemlock Creek to Hobson Creek in honour of J.B. Hobson, a mining engineer who opened up the Bullion Mine in the Cariboo around 1900.

flow into the river, which then runs into the North Thompson, north and east of Kamloops. The Clearwater River drains a large gold-bearing area and no doubt brings vast quantities of this gold down, depositing it in its own bars and banks and in those of the North Thompson River. In 1900 platinum was also discovered a short distance above Clearwater's confluence with the North Thompson, and it can still be found there. The Clearwater River remains an excellent area to pan and recover gold.

Hobson Creek (formerly Hemlock Creek)

★ ★ ★

Hobson Creek flows into Hobson Lake at the north end. It is a fair-sized creek that runs for approximately a kilometre on a slight grade up, and then for some distance above this point is a rushing torrent of water with a grade of over 10 percent.

The creek has been known to be gold bearing since around 1900. In 1922 new discoveries of placer gold were made on the creek at the north end of Clearwater Lake. At that time, transportation facilities were non-existent; consequently, little work was done here. When a small amount of work was done about two kilometres upstream from the mouth of the creek, some gold was recovered along the bed and banks. The old workings consist of tunnels, flumes, dams and ditches constructed to test the gravels. The area tested is on the creek's left bank and is considered to be a bench deposit rising above the creek bed. It is felt that this bench is an older channel of the creek. The miners opened up a bank some 45 to 60 metres (150 to 200 feet) high, and coarse gold as well as fine gold was recovered. Although the average values were not given in dollars or ounce amounts, it was stated that they were good. In 1930 prospecting was carried out approximately 4 kilometres (2.5 miles) above the mouth of Hobson Creek, and good values in gold were again recovered. Gold still exists here in good quantities.

Unfortunately, there is still no road access to Hobson Creek, and it is difficult to access by land.

Scotch Creek ✶

Scotch Creek flows into Shuswap Lake. The creek and its tributaries drain an area extending some 40 kilometres (25 miles) north of the lake. It is recorded that a considerable amount of gold was recovered here between 1880 and 1900. In 1885 gold was recovered approximately 16 kilometres (10 miles) upstream from the mouth of the creek. The gold was coarse pellets and nuggets found in the bars and banks. In 1933 the bench gravels were tested as far as 34 kilometres (21 miles) upstream from the mouth of Scotch Creek, and they indicated good paying gravels. These gravels, as well as evidence of old workings, still exist. About 19 kilometres (12 miles) from the creek's mouth, on the east side, there is evidence of an old channel 53 metres (175 feet) above the creek. This is where miners working by hand on the bedrock recovered some 1.7 kilograms (60 ounces) of gold in 1934. Historical records show that miners have also been successful when working the high banks on both sides of the creek.

The present creek has not been worked to any great extent. A re-concentration of gold from the old high channels can be found throughout the creek, and much fine gold occurs in the gravels at the

Scotch Creek Bridge, circa 1930.

mouth. Each year, successive runoffs bring new deposits of gold into Scotch Creek. The gold found here is heavy and bright in colour.

Sugar Lake ✳✳

On the Shuswap River, approximately five kilometres (three miles) below Sugar Lake, good values in gold have been found. This area has not been mined to any great extent, and the bars, banks and riverbed can be panned with good results.

A FISHY TALE

There is always a joker in every camp, and I remember a time when I was in the bush with five or six other prospectors—we were doing some staking work for one of the big mines—and this one guy was just a tease and a torment. You know, he would tie your boot laces together while you were asleep and just get up to anything he could think of and then laugh and titter at the results.

Well, this one day we had the woodstove going, and those little garden snakes used to come into the cabin we were in; they'd climb through holes in the floor and lie near the stove to keep warm. This fella, we found out, was terrified of snakes, and I stored this information away for future reference. In the meantime, we were still falling foul of his pranks and, I might tell you, getting a mite fed up with them.

Some time later, when we had a break, I said, "Let's go and get some trout." When you're in the bush like we were, you need to supplement the basic rations. So that's what we did. Well, I tell you, those fish were just delicious.

Anyhow, instead of throwing all of the bones and stuff away, I kept the heads and put them on some long sticks. While the joker was out of the cabin, I laid them on his pillow, some with just the lips showing and some with the eyes showing. When he came back in, I thought, "I'm gonna get you now, pest." The other guys were all sitting around, too, waiting for the fun. So I said to the joker, "Hey! What's that on your bed?"

"What do you mean?" he asked.

"I dunno," I said. "I thought I saw something moving on your pillow."

Well, he takes one look at his pillow, lets a great big yell outta' him, and takes off through the door like the devil himelf was chasing him. For once we had a good laugh at his expense.

A little while later he comes back to the cabin—by this time we had removed the "snakes"—stands in the door and asks us to pass him his pillow and sleeping bag. He would not come in at all and slept in his truck that night and every other night after that while we were in the camp. I don't know if he ever got cured of his trick-playing habits, but I'm sure he learned a lesson!

— Jim Lewis

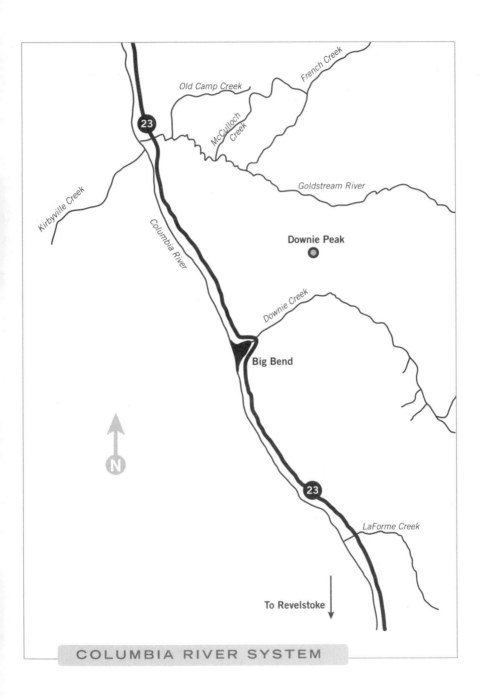

. . . .

Caines Creek ✶✶

Located north of Revelstoke, this creek has been known as a good gold-bearing creek since the 1860s, when gold was panned here by hand. The creek is approximately 11 kilometres (7 miles) long from the mouth to the forks, and each branch of the two forks is about 11 kilometres long, so it is a good-sized creek. About half a kilomere from the mouth of the creek is a canyon opening, below which are wide gravel banks. Above the canyon, the banks are 15 to 45 metres (50 to 150 feet) high, with sloping V-shaped sides and a few benches. Men doing hand mining in shallow diggings to bedrock were averaging 14 grams (half an ounce) per day per man, and the yield was occasionally as much as 43 grams (1.5 ounces) per day per man panning. Miners working on a hillside just above the canyon were also doing very well panning here. Approximately 1.5 to 2 kilometres (1 to 1.5 miles) above the canyon, good gold-bearing gravel was worked.

Four kilometres (2.5 miles) upstream, on the north side of the creek, a quartz ledge containing gold and silver was discovered in 1887. Severe flooding in that year took out the small dams and flumes that the miners had built. As this quartz ledge erodes, it no doubt contributes to the placer gold found in the creek.

For the eight kilometres (five miles) or so up to the forks, good recoveries of gold were being made on both sides of the creek. It is estimated that some $3 million in gold had been recovered from the creek by 1900, and subsequent work shows there are still good placer gold deposits that have never been touched. In 1933 a huge slide took a long stretch of the highway out, damaging three bridges; consequently, mining was postponed until late in the year. Since the Second World War, limited gold placer mining has been carried out on Caines Creek, and today it is an excellent area to pan and prospect.

Laforme Creek ✶✶

This creek, located about 13 kilometres (eight miles) south of Caines Creek, runs into the Columbia River approximately 32 kilometres (20 miles) north of Revelstoke. Placer gold has been panned on the creek for many years, and it remains a good location to pan to this day.

French Creek ✶✶

This creek has been an excellent gold-bearing source since 1900. With its adjoining creeks, it offers approximately 40 kilometres (25 miles) of good panning area. Nuggets as large as 85 grams (3 ounces) have been found along French Creek. At the headwaters of the creek, numerous gulches and ravines run in an east-west direction and have cut through the gold-bearing ore bodies in the area, often at right angles. In other places, there are outcrops of gold-bearing ore in the hillsides. Specimens from both of these occurring ores have proven to be rich with gold showing to the eye. This situation remains today, and gold is deposited in varying amounts each year into French Creek.

French Creek was discovered in the 1860s. In 1886 it was recorded as the source of gold coming into the Goldstream River, as it joins that river approximately 18 kilometres (11 miles) from the mouth. Gold in paying quantities had been discovered in both the high banks and in Goldstream River. In 1889 French Creek offered as much as 170 grams (6 ounces) of gold for every two metres (six feet) of ground worked. By 1893 good paying ground was being worked by four men, and applications for claims on the creek were being made. The following year at least 30 men were panning and recovering gold here. Inevitably, disputes arose between the partners and were not settled until late into the season. Old workings are visible along the creek and are excellent indications of where to pan.

In the early 1900s, miners were still making good recoveries in previously worked ground. Records show that by 1918 French Creek was the most important creek historically for its recorded output of gold. One miner lived and worked on the creek continuously from 1884 to well into the 1930s and remained self-sufficient, working alone, recovering gold all those years.

In the benches on the west side of French Creek, approximately a kilometre up from the Goldstream River, there are obvious indications of an old channel following an irregular course more or less parallel to the existing creek bed. From a casual inspection, it would appear that the creek has been forced east to its present position, occupying successive channels that in turn became blocked by boulders and slides of country rock. Records from 1922 state that the source of the creek's gold is this eroded old channel and also the veins in rock found in the upper area toward the headwaters.

Although French Creek has produced gold for decades, it has

not been all mined out or recovered. This is still a good creek for the present-day gold panner to investigate.

McCulloch Creek ✶✶

Approximately six kilometres (four miles) west of French Creek, McCulloch Creek also flows into the Goldstream River. A road leads upstream for nearly the full distance of the creek. Numerous small, unnamed creeks adjoining and flowing into it are also gold bearing.

By 1887 there was a great demand for prospectors, but not many were in the area. Good results were obtained on the creek in 1888, until some of the hoses they were using burst and it was too late in the season to obtain material for repairs. Litigation in 1893 stopped work altogether (though by 1896 the lawsuits were settled and people were once again working on the claims), and in 1895 a pumphouse was constructed, but unfortunately the pump never arrived because bad weather had made the trails impassable for animals with heavy loads.

In spite of these problems, the McCulloch Creek area was considered one of the best in the region for placer gold recovery. A lot of work was done by 1898 and a good deal of gold taken out. However, lack of machinery and transport facilities seriously hindered the work, and an incredibly wet season did not help the situation. In 1899 there were plans to work the creek on a larger scale, and in the early 1900s a new company bought out the previous owners and started working on the financing. However, they spent too much money doing the preparatory work ($16,000—a tremendous amount in those days) and not enough on mining.

By 1908 considerable work was being accomplished, despite slides causing extensive damage to installations, and gold was once again being recovered in paying quantities. The records of 1912 show that only the richer ground was worked due to the shortness of the season and the

Miners' cabin, McCulloch Creek, circa 1890.

high cost of obtaining supplies, if they could be obtained at all. In 1915 shafts were sunk to bedrock, but this was again doomed to failure as the lack of pumping machinery drove the miners out. In 1916 several individuals were working the creek making good recoveries of gold, but by 1922 placer mining was nearly at a standstill, not for the lack of gold in the creek, but due to the interest generated by hardrock mining in the area. The upper portion of McCulloch Creek continued to produce good placer gold for the few people working the area. In September of 1926, one group of miners that started washing gravel reported that the results were encouraging, as the gold was coarse and easy to recover.

After the Second World War, not much placer mining was done, as miners and mining companies were concentrating on hardrock claims and ore bodies.

One miner, working by hand with no equipment, took out $500 of gold in six weeks. With the price of gold at that time varying between $16 and $18 per ounce, this amount was equal to 879 grams (31 ounces)— a nice-sized "poke" by any standard.

Old Camp Creek ✶✶

This creek flows into the Goldstream River north of Revelstoke, approximately eight kilometres (five miles) from McCulloch Creek. Gold has been found on Old Camp Creek from its mouth to its headwaters. In the late 1800s, flumes were installed to bring water for the purpose of hydraulic mining. By 1902 approximately five kilometres (three miles) of flume had been constructed, and the miners working the top gravels obtained excellent results. By 1909 only a small amount of work was being done by a few individuals at the mouth of the creek. A lack of facilities and capital required to move in machinery, with no roads or rail transportation to the area, were the biggest problems faced. The records of 1915 show that no development of any consequence had taken place on the creek. Although heavy gold had been found on the rimrock of the area, the bedrock had never been worked.

Just above the falls at the upper end of the canyon, ground sluicing recovered over 3,175 grams (112 ounces) of gold in 1932 and 3,147 grams (111 ounces) in 1933. Subsequently, rich ground was discovered just half a kilometre above the canyon, where all the work was done with a shovel and a wheelbarrow. Later that year, a handmade split-lumber sluice box measuring 30 metres (100 feet) long was constructed and used. Gold-bearing gravel was obtained from an old run of gravel on bedrock above the level of the present stream and adjoining the eastern rim of the creek; some 7,087 grams (250 ounces) of gold was recovered here. Fifteen metres (50 feet) upstream on the same side, good results were also found on bedrock some 2 metres (7 feet) lower than the area mentioned above.

The Old Camp Creek area still contains gold in good quantity, so it is well worth investigating.

Downie Creek ✶✶

This is a large, long creek that drains an extensive area north of

Revelstoke. Gold-bearing tributaries flow into it, and as early as 1886 miners had asked that a mining recorder's office be located at Downie Creek because it was central to other gold-bearing creeks in the area.

Goldstream River ✷✷

The Goldstream River has long been known as a placer stream. It flows into the Columbia River north of Revelstoke and drains French and McCulloch Creeks as well as others in the area. The bars and banks of the Goldstream River from the mouth upstream to the headwaters have been worked with good success during periods of low water.

Kirbyville Creek ✷✷

This creek was discovered to have placer gold at its mouth, where it joins the Columbia River from the west, close to where the Goldstream River enters the Columbia. This discovery was made in 1886, when three groups of miners started to prospect and work the creek. The 1893 records show that two men working on a bench above the mouth of Kirbyville Creek during high-water periods, and on the Goldstream River during low-water periods, got good results.

Due to the close proximity of these two streams, miners had a choice of the two areas to work. By 1893 10 miners were actively prospecting and panning on Kirbyville Creek; 20 men were actively employed for part of the season on the Goldstream River.

In 1895 only development work and very little mining was done on Kirbyville Creek. At that time, miners had to pack in supplies on trails approximately 100 to 116 kilometres (60 to 70 miles) long. This was extremely costly and time-consuming. In 1898 records report that "colours" of gold could be found anywhere on the surface from both banks, starting at the mouth of Kirbyville Creek and going upstream. High values have also been found on this creek on bedrock.

Hydraulic mining at Big Bend, circa 1900.

After 1905 and up to 1912, little work was done here, and by 1915 hardly any mining was being carried out at all. During the period of the First World War, however, several individuals were making good money working near the mouth of the creek.

There is a privately owned property at the mouth of Kirbyville Creek, so permission must be obtained prior to gaining access.

BIG FEET

Many times—matter of fact, more times than I can recount or recall—people have asked me if I've seen any unusual occurrences while travelling in wilderness areas. In particular, Sasquatch hunters have approached me and asked if I have ever seen anything remotely resembling a Sasquatch. Well, the physical being I have never seen. However, on one trip a friend and I were going into a real remote area. It really wasn't a road anymore—you could never put a vehicle through there. We were about 400 yards away from a lake, with a small creek flowing from the lake down into the river, and were on a height of land walking along when all of a sudden we smelled the godawfullest stink any person ever ran into. It smelled like rotten fish and rotten meat combined, if you can imagine that! My partner said to me, "There could be a bear here," and I replied, "You're right." We had packsacks and gear, and we both had rifles for our own protection, so we kept walking along the trail, keeping a wary eye out for whatever was in the area. We walked about 100 feet, and suddenly the smell wasn't there anymore. There was fresh air again, and so we kept walking.

We walked about another four miles before we finally made camp that day, and then we were working the area for three days, prospecting it and looking at different rocks and taking samples and doing a general overlay of the place. There were some good prospects in there, but it was so remote that it would cost a lot of money to develop it. Anyway, that's neither here nor there. The substance of this thing is that when we came back out, I said to my partner, "Oh, we're coming to that area where the smell was. I wonder if it's still there. It must be a carcass because nothing would smell like that otherwise." So when we came to this area, we approached it with caution. We knew exactly where it was because on our way in we had noted the location real well—and we were watching and listening, but when we arrived, there was no smell of any kind.

Well, I don't really want to perpetuate the legend of the Sasquatch or of any other kind of subhuman being. However, there was nothing to explain what we had smelled and nothing to explain the tracks we saw in that area. Neither one of us could say exactly what made them, and both of us were experienced in the bush. Over the years I've seen pictures—not in books or magazines, but actual pictures taken by one individual prospector—of unusual tracks. He had walked on the crust of hard snow alongside where it seemed a super-human being had walked. These tracks were approximately 12 to 14 inches deep, approximately 12 to 14 inches long and about 6 inches wide. They were just like the tracks we saw in the soft ground by the creek and were definitely not bear tracks or any tracks we recognized. However, no Sasquatch has ever bothered me and I've certainly never run into one of them. Possibly there's such a thing and possibly there isn't—I've no evidence either way, positive or negative.

—Jim Lewis

Big Bend ✷✷

This area of the Columbia River has been worked for placer gold with good results. In 1909 20 men worked all winter preparing for the spring mining season. In later years, placer mining during times of low water has been done on all of the Columbia River north of Revelstoke, with good results being obtained from its banks and bars.

PART
IV

THE OKANAGAN
AND THE KOOTENAYS

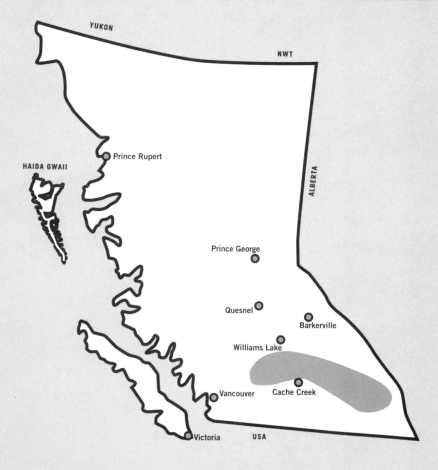

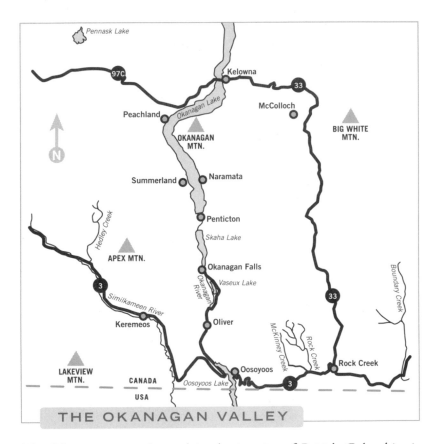

THE OKANAGAN VALLEY

The Okanagan area, located in the interior of British Columbia, is home to vineyards, lakes and hot summer days. The area not only produces world-famous wines, but also luscious juicy peaches and other summer fruits. It is also the home of the mysterious monster of Lake Okanagan—Ogopogo.

There is yet another rewarding pastime to enjoy in these beautiful parts of BC if you enjoy fun, sun and the great outdoors (and sometimes wet feet)—gold panning. This section outlines some of our favourite areas and those where we have enjoyed the greatest success.

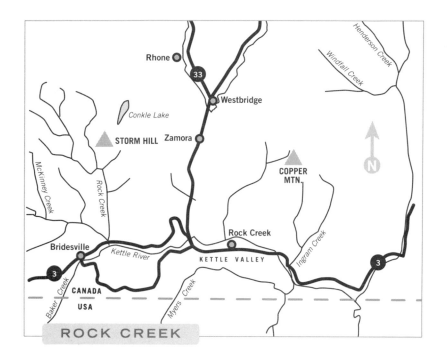

Rock Creek ★

The small village of Rock Creek is located on the Crowsnest Highway 3, between Osoyoos and Greenwood in Boundary Country, just north of the Canada–United States border. Rock Creek itself is one of the more famous placer creeks in the southern Okanagan region. The history of this gold-bearing creek dates back to around 1860. A Mr. Beame was one of the first miners to find and recover gold on this creek. From approximately 1860 to 1869, a series of gold rushes began with an estimated 5,000 hopeful miners descending on the area. Later, copper, silver, lead and zinc ores were mined, but gold was the lure that initially brought the miners to the area. Old records show that the area was, and still is, rich in gold that is carried down from the nearby Mount Baldy area in the annual runoff. The famous phrase, "There's gold in them thar hills!" still rings true.

From June to November 1860, over 2,300 kilograms (83,000 ounces) of gold (then priced at $16.00 per fine ounce) was officially recovered— and it's quite likely that a lot more was recovered but not reported! The largest nuggets were over 28 grams (1 ounce). Only the surface was worked as pumps and the other devices, such as water wheels, had to be constructed from wood on the spot, and miners could not obtain any equipment because it was unavailable.

One attempt at sinking a shaft was made near the mouth of Rock Creek on the south side of lease No. 58. Along the rimrock opposite this shaft, several thousand dollars worth of coarse gold nuggets were found. Work done on the west side of Lots 73 and 67 strongly suggests the presence of an old channel forming a semicircle some 250 metres (800 feet) long commencing on Lot 67 and ending near an old tunnel on Lot 73. Some coarse gold was located from this old channel bedrock some 6 metres (20 feet) above the present creek bed in 1916. Lot 58 is located at the mouth of the canyon where the valley widens and where the concentration of gold would naturally occur after being carried through the narrow gorge. As far as experienced gold panners can tell, the creek ground and high banks have only been superficially worked, and the lower creek strata have not been worked at all. On Lots 74 and 76, rimrock with very good paying gravel was found about 37 metres (120 feet) above the present creek. Lots 74 and 76 and the northern part of Lot 58 consist of a flat bench about half a kilometre wide and about 75 metres (250 feet) higher than the creek. The finding of high rimrock has led to the conclusion that an old channel of the creek once flowed from the northwest corner of Lot 76 to the northeast corner of Lot 58 and that a change of watercourse was caused by glacial debris.

Similar conditions have been proven on Lot 55 and are likely to exist in places along the entire creek so that examining the banks is recommended where similar conditions exist. On Lot 52, work has demonstrated possible old high channels, and in all likelihood the creek at one time cut across Lot 57. On Lot 65, some prospecting had been done at the upper entrance to a canyon where the creek bed widens out to over 100 metres. The ground appears never to have been worked. Only the gold from the more easily worked alluvial gravels has been checked and worked, and there remain long and important stretches of the creek gravels and old channels higher up from the present creek that have never been touched.

Nearly all the gold is coarse and rusty in colour—occasionally lemon-coloured nuggets have been found. On the older maps, the tributaries of Rock Creek were named as the North and South Forks. They are now called Jolly Creek and McKinney Creek, respectively.

Jolly Creek ✶✶

It was difficult to finance work on the old channel on Jolly Creek in 1932, so very little work was actually done. The map referred to in 1932 shows the work that was done and indicates that very attractive values were found on a wide and flat floor of the old channel, about 8 metres (25 feet) above the present creek bed. Denver Bar has about the same elevation and was at one time possibly part of the old streambed. It is suggested the old channel worked its way backward and forward, and later Jolly Creek cut across. Good paying gravel may be found in the present creek just below the intersections. A small part of the present creek gravels were worked in previous years and very good recoveries made, with especially good finds made on Lots 73 and 55. Glacial debris was most likely the cause of the creek changing direction.

McKinney Creek ✶✶

On McKinney Creek (old south fork of Rock Creek), about a kilometre above the McKinney Creek Road crossing, miners working by hand obtained good results. They recovered fairly coarse gold on benches about a metre above the present stream on the east side. About three kilometres (two miles) upstream near the mouth of Rice Creek, some fine gold was recovered on a high point of bedrock. About 150 metres (500 feet) above the mouth of Rice Creek, coarse gold was found on bedrock. This is on a flat area about a kilometre long and some 60 metres (200 feet) wide just above a small canyon. On a low bench 3 metres (10 feet) above the present creek, the gravel varied from 2 to 3 metres (6 to 10 feet) deep and cemented gravel was found lying close to bedrock. On the east side, a cut dugout suggests that an old channel flowed along this side and on the opposite side of the present streambed.

Disputes between claim owners and the miners who leased from them, and the lack of financing caused the claims not to be worked at many intervals over the years. Financing was a particularly big problem and remains the same today for placer operations.

Boundary Creek ✶✶

Long known as a good placer creek, Boundary Creek was exceptionally rich in place gold south of the falls. Gold was first discovered here in 1858 or 1859, and this creek was worked intermittently by hand methods during the early years. Placer mining was carried out on Boundary Creek from its junction with the Kettle River upstream for approximately three kilometres (two miles).

Norwegian Creek ✶

Norwegian Creek flows into Boundary Creek about three kilometres (two miles) upstream from Midway, and it was once believed that Boundary Creek did not contain any gold above Norwegian Creek. This theory was disproved when coarse gold was found along the edge of the flats above Norwegian Creek on Boundary Creek. Boundary Creek flows into the Kettle River below Midway. There are still areas here today that have never been worked and gold is still recovered.

At the mouth of Norwegian Creek, test pits were dug and gold recovered. These pits were tested on the Creek and along the flat on the east side downstream and good values were found.

Cedar Creek ✱ ✱

Cedar Creek flows into the west side of the Kettle River, some 19 kilometres (12 miles) north of Westbridge. Above the first canyon there are old workings on a bench about two metres (six feet) above the present creek bed and also about three kilometres (two miles) farther west upstream. The gold panned along the creek was found to be fine and well rounded, pointing to the fact that it had travelled a long distance. There is a deep depression about a kilometre long and 150 metres (500 feet) wide formed below the first canyon, which, in turn, has formed a catch basin for gold. Nothing but superficial work has been done here.

Steel bridge over Cedar Creek, 1900. VANCOUVER PUBLIC LIBRARY 846

CPR tracks along Kamloops Lake, one mile west of Cherry Creek.

Cherry Creek ✶ ✶

By 1892 miners were still recovering gold by hand on Cherry Creek. The reported production in 1893 from this creek was $4,000 (with gold at $18 per fine ounce). It is quite likely that another quantity of equal value went unreported that year because the people involved wanted to keep it secret. The following year, some $3,200 was reported.

As early as 1876, placer miners were working Cherry Creek, panning and using hand-sawn wooden rockers. The yield via pan was approximately 14 grams (half an ounce) per day per man. In 1877 panners were averaging over 28 grams (1 ounce) per day per man. From the mouth upstream for several miles, people were getting good results. On a bench some 15 metres (50 feet) above the creek and several kilometres upstream, nuggets weighing 227 grams (8.5 ounces), 170 grams (6 ounces) and 71 grams (2.5 ounces) were found. Very good prospects were discovered on Falls Creek, a small tributary of Cherry Creek. Some 283 grams (10 ounces) of gold per man per day was being recovered from the bars in the main Cherry Creek. There are numerous quartz ledges on Cherry Creek that are gold bearing, and there is no doubt that these feed gold to the creek each and every year.

Falls Creek Area *

There is evidence of early placer mining near Falls Creek. In 1901, despite exceptionally high water levels and few miners working on Cherry Creek, gold was still being recovered. Above Falls Creek, Cherry Creek is wide and the gravel is small and easily worked. About a kilometre below Falls Creek, work was being done on the left bank. One man was working alone and recovering gold. Three kilometres (two miles) farther down the creek, people were working the streambed.

By 1920 there was little mining activity on Cherry Creek except for placer leases being worked on the creek and on Whiteman Creek mentioned below. In 1922 there was placer work carried on near Monashee Mountain on Cherry Creek, and some hydraulic mining was done until late June.

The benches above Falls Creek were being prospected with good results in 1925, and miners were exploring the possibility of pre-glacial channels in the area. By 1930

Over the hill and east of the Monashee Mill House lies the placer ground where A.L. Marsh single handedly drove a 760-metre (2,500-foot) tunnel in a vain attempt to reach bedrock in the bottom of the gulch. Marsh came to Cherry Creek in 1883 from San Francisco, where he had lost a large fortune in a business venture, a fortune he had acquired from mining in Nevada. Convinced that a second fortune awaited him if he could reach bedrock, he did the work himself. Commencing in 1898, he laboured in driving this tunnel for 12 years before he found that the first timbers he had put in were beginning to rot and fall in, and he had to abandon the project. For the first 45 metres (150 feet), the tunnel runs through a slide area, then for about 50 metres (175 feet) through blue clay. The rest is coarse gravel with a few boulders. By 1913 Mr. Marsh was 70 years of age and still had unfailing faith in Cherry Creek as a gold producer. Through the years he worked there, he recovered enough gold to keep himself fed and clothed, though he failed to reach a bonanza.

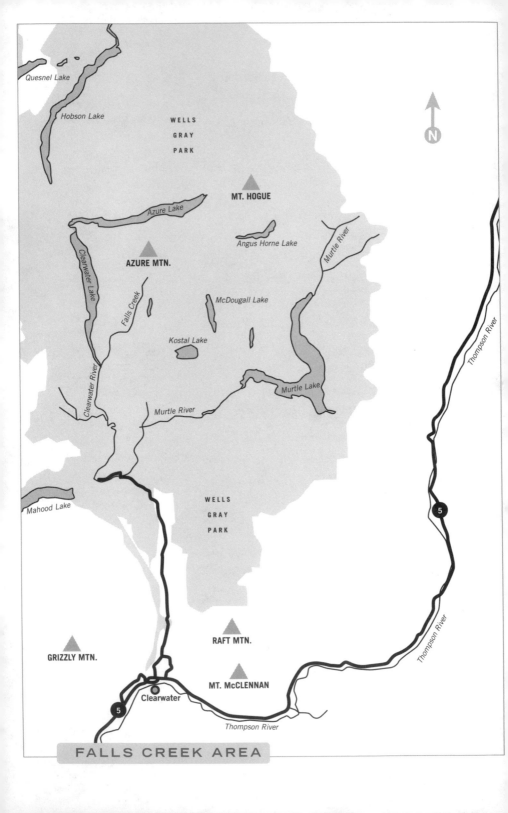

Quesnel Lake

Hobson Lake

WELLS
GRAY
PARK

MT. HOGUE

Azure Lake

Angus Horne Lake

Murtle River

AZURE MTN.

Clearwater Lake

Falls Creek

McDougall Lake

Kostal Lake

Murtle Lake

Murtle River

Clearwater River

Thompson River

Mahood Lake

WELLS
GRAY
PARK

5

Thompson River

RAFT MTN.

GRIZZLY MTN.

MT. McCLENNAN

Clearwater

5

Thompson River

FALLS CREEK AREA

there was again very little activity in the placer claims as most miners were more interested in pursuing veins in the rock of the area. In 1931 only minor operations by individual prospectors were being carried on. By 1935 several individuals were working on Cherry Creek and recovering gold in paying quantities. From the Second World War onward, no placer mining was carried on to any extent in the Falls Creek area.

Whiteman Creek ✶✶

By 1915 preliminary work to start hydraulic placer mining on Whiteman Creek was underway. Water sufficient for this work would have to be ditched and piped for approximately 2 kilometres (1.5 miles). Staking and preparatory work as well as prospecting was being done in 1920; however, no mining of any consequence was being done. Placer leases were being staked in 1921. Whiteman Creek is still a good area to pan today as very little has been done.

Fourth of July Creek ✶✶

Located in the Grand Forks area, Fourth of July Creek has long been known as a placer gold creek. It was discovered in 1859 by American prospectors crossing into Canada and panning the creeks en route. There are several tributaries flowing into Fourth of July Creek from the northwest, such as Taylor (or Skeff) Creek, May Creek and Gibbs Creek. May Creek has been found to be gold bearing. Skeff Creek has old workings on it. A short distance above the area where Chinese miners worked on Skeff Creek in the late 19th century, placer gold has been found.

It is a very small creek and has very little water during the drier seasons. There is an area of Skeff Creek that has not been mined near its headwaters. This area and May Creek, as well as Fourth of July Creek, are all good bets for panning. Chinese workings are well indicated by piles of rock (sometimes resembling rock fences) metres away from the actual workings.

Seward Creek ★★

Situated on the west side of Okanagan Lake, Seward Creek has long been known as a gold-bearing creek. Part of it runs through a First Nations reserve, and permission to pan must be obtained before proceeding. Gold was discovered in this creek in the late 1800s, and it was never mined out. The high banks called hill claims were checked and found to be gold bearing. Very little actual mining was done on this creek in the early years, but two placer claims were being worked above the reserve area in 1893. By 1894 the workings had improved, and miners were recovering gold in paying quantities. A year later, six men were working on the creek bed and banks with good results. There were several Chinese miners downstream from the first group mentioned and they were recovering gold.

Siwash Creek ★★★

Some 2.5 kilometres (1.5 miles) from the mouth of Siwash Creek on Okanagan Lake, veins bearing free gold were found and undoubtedly enriched the creek area. In 1915 some hydraulic mining yeilded an excellent recovery of gold. The area worked was just above the First Nations reserve on Siwash Creek, also called Naswhito Creek. Approximately three kilometres (two miles) upstream from the mouth of the creek, some work was done to build flumes and pipelines to wash the gravel. By 1930 the major activity had stopped, but individual miners were recovering gold in paying quantities. Very little placer mining was carried on in the years after the Second World War, and Siwash is still a very good area for gold panning.

Peachland Creek ★

Peachland Creek, formerly called Deep Creek, has been a known placer creek since before the turn of the 19th century. Through the years, miners working by hand recovered gold in paying quantities from the mouth of the stream to its headwaters.

Trout Creek ✶✶

Similar to Deep Creek in that the placer mining was done by individuals, Trout Creek was worked from the mouth of the creek upstream, and miners recovered gold in paying quantities. There were no large operations on this creek, and gold is still being panned by individuals here. The north fork of Trout Creek also proved to be fruitful from the bench gravels on the west side of the creek. Minimal work was done here after miners discovered this area in 1933, so it could very well hold unknown treasures.

Mission Creek ✶✶

In 1876 miners were working on Mission Creek and making good recoveries. All mining in these years was being done by hand, as there were few roads and absolutely no machinery available. By 1877 miners were working the banks by packing the gold-bearing gravels to the creek and washing the gold out with rockers and pans. There were some attempts to bring the water to the benches from upstream in order to work the benches from the mouth of the creek and along its watercourse. The creek has produced good gold from its headwaters to its mouth.

Past the 16-kilometre (10-mile) mark, very little gold has been found in the creek. The first 16 kilometres of the creek are best from the mouth upstream. High gold values were recorded on this stream in past years. In 1933 and 1934, miners were still working by hand, but they were making good returns for the amount of work done. Since the Second World War, very little organized placer mining has been done, so the creek is an excellent area to pan today.

Woods Lake ✶✶

Placer gold on Woods Lake (between Vernon and Kelowna) was first discovered on an old high channel to the east of the lake, and gold was recovered from the area just above bedrock. This old high channel is approximately 1.5 kilometres (1 mile) long, 1.5 kilometres (1 mile) wide and some 60 metres (200 feet) thick. Old tunnels were driven here, the lowest approximately two metres (seven feet) above bedrock, and coarse placer gold was recovered here. About 250 metres (800 feet) below the leases, the CN Railway traverses the east side of Woods Lake. This area is located about 1.5 kilometres (1 mile) east of Woods Lake and a considerable amount of placer gold was found here. Prospecting continued on into 1935 and gold was still being recovered. In 1936, it was found that gold-bearing gravels were located high up on the eastern hillside flanking Woods Lake. These gravels are at an elevation of about 900 metres (3,000 feet) and are known to extend from near Clark Creek northwards for a distance of about three kilometres (two miles).

The gold-bearing gravels lie above weathered bedrock. They are definitely stream-lain and represent part of an ancient draining system. The gold is quite pure and reddish in colour, and some pieces are flattened pellets the size of match heads or smaller. In some areas, the gold in the gravels is fine, and in other areas pellets predominate.

After the Second World War, the Woods Lake area was forgotten and has not been worked to any extent since. Today, this is an excellent area to explore and pan, but always remember to consult local maps to determine the best access points.

Harris Creek ✶✶

Flowing into the broad Lumby-Long Lake Valley at a point approximately 6 kilometres (3.5 miles) southwest of Lumby, Harris Creek's headwaters are in the Buck Hills and flow northwest some 23 kilometres (14 miles) to its confluence with Nicklen Creek. From this point Harris

Creek flows north and east to the Shuswap River. Below the principal tributary, McCauley (Gold) Creek, a distance of some 12 kilometres (7.5 miles), the creek flows in a flat-bottomed valley. Immediately below the mouth of Nicklen Creek is a section of canyon about 30 metres (100 feet) wide and 183 metres (600 feet) long where, from here, the creek enters the valley. A prominent gravel bench level flanks the Lumby Valley at a height of about 600 metres (2,000 feet) and is preserved for some 10 kilometres (6 miles) of the Harris Creek Valley.

In these gravels, fairly coarse gold is found—heavy and well-worn nuggets up to 50 grams (1.75 ounces). The gold is dark in colour and polished. There is very little black sand associated with this gold. Boulder slag has been exposed in the old hydraulic pit on the west side of Harris Creek Canyon and definitely overlies the gravel in the old channel. This area was worked very little before 1931, when it was prospected by two miners who went on to discover the old channel in 1936.

The first 13 kilometres (8 miles) from the mouth upstream and between Harris and Jones Creek have been prospected. On the southwest side, approximately 7 kilometres (4.5 miles) from the mouth of Harris Creek, some good results were found 6 metres (20 feet) above the creek from the rimrock areas. On ground about a kilometre below, or downstream, from this locality, very shallow digging shows that a rock rim of similar gravels and gold was found, but no real testing was done. Testing in the bed of the creek consisted of panning on the surface; no pits have been dug more than about a metre deep.

The original discovery in 1936 is on the east side of the creek at the head of a small canyon (looking upstream) just below the mouth of Nicklen Creek. Three hundred and forty grams (12 ounces) of coarse gold was taken from surface among large boulders over an area some 5 by 15 metres (15 by 50 feet). This remnant of the channel is not worked out, and coarse gold can still be panned here. Prospectors moved across the channel to the west side of Harris Creek and recovered 397 grams

(14 ounces) of gold before optioning the ground to a man who did not pursue the venture further. The lowest part of this old channel is 6 metres (20 feet) above the present creek bed and about 3 metres (10 feet) wide. About 6 metres above this, the channel is 18 metres (60 feet) wide with steep walls.

Jones Creek ✻✻

Some 150 metres (500 feet) west of Harris Creek, the ground slopes gradually toward Jones Creek. Gold has been recovered 3 to 8 metres (10 to 25 feet) above the lowest gutter and in the top 4.5 metres (15 feet) of gravel starting some 6 metres (20 feet) above the present creek bed. On Jones Creek, 2 kilometres (1.5 miles) west, the old channel has been searched for gold and it is plain that the present Jones Creek has cut through rim rock and formed a canyon to flow through. Immediately south of this, there are gold-bearing gravels, as at this point both Jones Creek and Harris Creek are at the same elevation and the old channel would be approximately 30 metres (100 feet) deep.

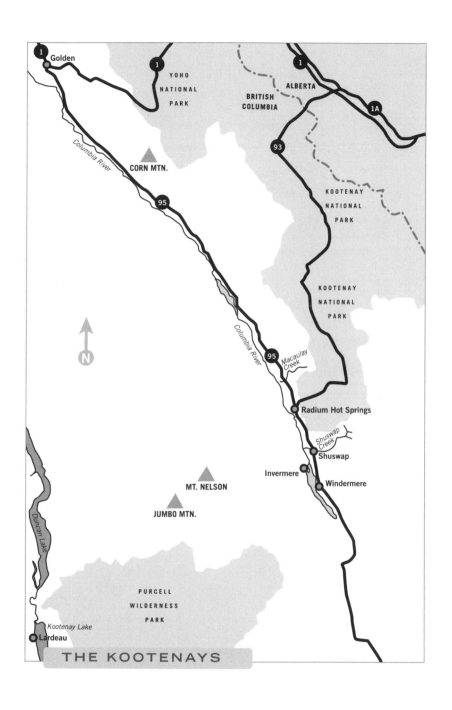

THE KOOTENAYS

. . . .

The Kootenay area, regarded by many as an extension of the Okanagan Valley, is yet another area with a rich history of gold-rush mining and is rich in minerals and gold. Many mines—both silver and gold, as well as copper, lead and zinc—have operated in the region over the years. Today, prospectors may be pleasantly surprised by what they find here.

Putnam Creek ✶✶

A small easterly flowing creek 19 kilometres (12 miles) north of Lumby, Putnam Creek has its headwaters in mountainous country. They flow in a narrow valley some eight kilometres (five miles) in length to enter the broad-terraced Trinity Valley. Gold was first discovered on this creek in October 1936. Gold was discovered from the mouth upstream, and bedrock is not exposed in the first 2 kilometres (1.5 miles) below the canyon. The gravels covering the bedrock are not deep, but above the canyon the gravels are deeper. The gold here is heavy and well rounded, and black sand is present. Very little testing or other work has ever been done here, and it is an excellent creek to pan and recover gold.

Perry Creek (Fort Steele Area) ✶

Perry Creek was one of the first great placer creeks discovered by miners in the 1850s and 1860s, and proved to be a very productive gold-bearing creek—though many miners left the area in the late 1850s and early 1860s to try their luck in the Cariboo goldfields. The rich paying gravels found on Perry Creek are shallow below the falls, and gold was recovered from high points of rock for some 13 kilometres (8 miles) upstream from the falls leading the miners to believe that this creek indeed is very rich in gold. In 1880 good paying gravels were being washed below the falls from the creek bed by a small group working by hand and without any machinery available to them. The upper portion of the creek above the falls was not being worked at that time. Lack of water in 1883 stopped all work on Perry Creek, and no mining was done. By 1887 miners were digging shafts down through the gravel in attempts to reach bedrock above the falls area—but they were unsuccessful thanks to water problems and lack of pumps.

Apart from the one company working there in 1879, a few individual miners were working and recovering good values in gravel. Excessive flooding in 1893 caused all work to stop on this creek as all the miners' previous preparatory work had been washed away by the high water. By 1915 placer mining had stopped and only hard rock veins in the area were being worked on. By 1934 only one group was working on Perry Creek, but they were still recovering gold in paying quantities. After the Second World War, placer activity did not resume, and gold remains on this creek to this day.

Palmer Box Creek ✶✶

Known as a good placer gold–bearing creek from the 1870s to the present day, Palmer Box Creek had very rich yields in the past and was never mined out. Shallow diggings were worked on in 1876, but the scarcity of water hindered operations. The following year, water conditions were no better and only one small area was worked briefly, but its yield of gold was very good. Chinese miners were working the area in 1887 and 1888 recovering gold in good paying quantities in relation to the work done. In 1889 sluicing using wheelbarrows and sluice boxes was being carried on with good results. Gold has been recovered from the mouth upstream on this creek but was never mined out. The area remains good for panning to this day.

Erie Creek ✶

Gold was accidentally discovered on Erie Creek, the north fork of the Salmo River, in 1902. Two men were digging a well on the bank of the river for their cabin when they struck flour gold in very good quantity. They were able to work for quite a spell before the secret was let out. A mini gold rush ensued, with 49 leases on claims recorded. The original two men had staked a claim as soon as they discovered the gold-bearing gravels and before others found out their secret. This area is at the canyon just below where Whiskey Creek flows in on the north side of the river where there is an old channel containing well-washed water-worn gravel. The gold is fairly coarse and well worn, and the largest pieces weighed approximately seven grams (one-quarter of an ounce).

Whiskey Creek ✶✶

At the mouth of Whiskey Creek, gold was being recovered from the creek and banks in good quantities. By 1926 one man had built a small suction dredge and moved it to the north fork of the Salmo River (Cree Creek) about a kilometre upstream from the confluence with the main river. Unfortunately for this miner, after a very brief trial period a sudden burst of high water carried the dredge downstream where it was smashed beyond repair. Placer mining was never carried out to any extent in the area as miners concentrated their efforts in the gold-bearing veins of hard rock.

Pend D'Oreille River ✶✶

On the Pend D'Oreille River, placer values were known by the turn of the 20th century and some prospecting had been done before this period. By 1915 miners had been working the veins for gold and were saving less than 50 percent thanks to their crude milling process. A large pond of the tailings from this area is known to have a large concentration of gold, so this would be well worth panning today.

A group of men at the Lucky Jack mine in the Lardeau shortly after its discovery, 1900.

Lardeau Creek ★★★

Lardeau Creek is located above Trout Lake. Approximately 2 kilometres (1.5 miles) up the creek from the lake, some placer mining was carried out as late as 1939 with good results being obtained by hand methods. This area was never extensively mined and remains a very good area to pan for gold today.

Wild Horse and Boulder Creeks ★★★

The source of the gold in Wild Horse Creek is believed to be of local origin and derived from the veins of gold-bearing materials that outcrop along the creek. Gold has been found from the mouth of the stream up for a distance of some 32 kilometres (20 miles).

By 1875 a number of hill and bank claims had been staked, and miners were prospecting the creek banks and bars and recovering gold. On the southeast side of the creek miners were working and recovering good results by washing the banks with high-pressure streams of water

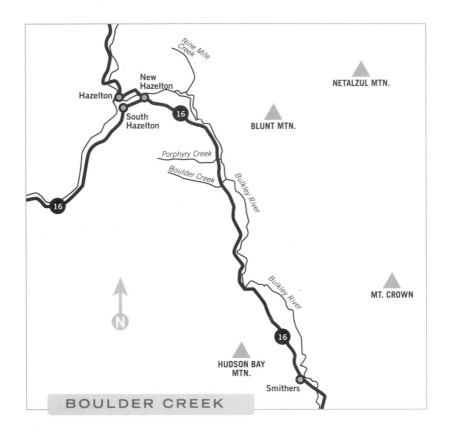

Nine Mile Creek

New Hazelton

Hazelton

South Hazelton

16

NETALZUL MTN.

BLUNT MTN.

Porphyry Creek

Boulder Creek

Bulkley River

Bulkley River

MT. CROWN

N

16

HUDSON BAY MTN.

Smithers

BOULDER CREEK

using monitors. On the opposite side of the creek, miners in a separate group were working, also with good results. The water for this type of mining had to be ditched for some distance in order to work the high banks. By 1880 the claims worked were paying very good dividends to the miners. Both sides of the creek were being worked in 1882, but low water in 1883 slowed the work considerably and not much mining was done (what little was done, however, paid well). By 1884 very high water inhibited work. Arguments between the railroad companies and the size of their land grants, plus the debate over whether miners could mine creeks and banks on those land grants, were heating up, which also stopped some prospecting. The arguments were eventually settled and work progressed in the following years.

By 1885 low water again hindered mining. In 1877 there were fewer miners working the creek; however, the yield of gold was very good. By this time, some miners had spent many years here and stated that the creek was still very productive. One miner who was unable to clean out his sluices due to an early freeze-up estimated that there was at least $15,000 worth of gold in his sluices (gold at that time was valued at $14.00 per fine ounce). When he did clean out his sluices the following year, it was found that he had underestimated his gold recovery by a fair amount.

Low water in 1889 again slowed things down and not much mining was accomplished. Gold was being recovered more by hand work and washing with rockers, not by hydraulic methods. New mining plants were being constructed by 1893, and work progressed after the railroad companies and the BC government had reached agreements regarding surface rights and miners were granted claims in the area. But in 1894, landslides hampered the miners' efforts, carrying away the ditches and flumes necessary to bring water to the higher ground. Good paying gravels were found in the vicinity of Victoria Gulch, but excessive flooding and landslides meant that work was confined to prospecting and hand-mining methods. Gold had risen in price to $17.60 per fine ounce. By 1895 this creek was considered the longest known placer mining creek in the area and was still paying very good dividends for the work being done. Little work, other than assessment work, was being done on the creek in 1896.

There is a bank about 900 metres (3,000 feet) high on the side of the creek that has been washed from 2 to 244 metres (6 to 800 feet) away from the creek. This bank was almost vertical and contained good values in gold. On the south side of the creek, just below this bank, very good results have been recovered. Farther downstream is a canyon where a number of other miners worked small claims and enjoyed good results.

By 1898 the creek was still producing very well and was far from being mined out. Many new recoveries of placer gold were made in 1898 and although it was considered the oldest mining project in the Kootenays, it was still very productive as long as excessive water, or lack of water, did not hamper operations. By 1901 Chinese miners were doing very well in previously worked ground. The other miners were mainly engaged in hardrock mining doing tunnels and sinking shafts on vein material. By 1902 the creek was still being worked by miners with good success and it is stated that individuals were working by hand and doing well. By 1903 miners were still getting good results on this creek and had gone to considerable expense to open up the banks and recover gold. Unfortunately, 1904 was a very dry year, and by 1915 placer mining had nearly ceased except for small groups of Chinese miners using rockers and shovelling by hand. With the First World War in progress, there was insufficient man power to work the creek areas, but renewed interest in 1918 once again proved that this creek had not been depleted of its gold.

By 1919 renewed interest in placer gold mining once again swept the area and virgin ground on the west side of the creek was found. However, an unusually dry season and the resulting shortage of water caused the operation to cease early in the spring. The gold being recovered was fairly coarse and of high grade—and the amount recovered was very satisfactory to the miners involved. By 1933 in the area from the mouth of Wild Horse Creek to above where Boulder Creek joins it, people were still working and recovering gold. No extensive working on Wild Horse Creek had been attempted above the mouth of Boulder Creek. On Wild Horse Creek, the limited amount of prospecting done may well account for the fact that not much gold was ever recovered in the stream.

Coarse gold was still being recovered on Wild Horse Creek and on Boulder Creek in 1934. By 1950 some attempts were being made to resume placer mining; however, prolonged high water hampered all efforts to resume working. Very little work had been done between 1934 and 1950 due to the Second World War and other factors.

By 1953 one man was still working his leases on Wild Horse Creek, approximately five kilometres (three miles) upstream from the mouth of the creek. By 1957 four leases at the mouth of Fisher Creek were being worked and some 9,000 metres (10,000 yards) of gravel were processed, producing coarse gold.

In 1958, due to the property having been sold to new interests, exploratory drilling for good gold deposits was being carried out and by 1961 gold was still being recovered in good quantities for the small amount of material processed. The year 1962 saw approximately 5,500 metres (6,000 yards) of material washed from the west bank of the river at the mouth of Fisher Creek (on Wild Horse Creek) and a good amount of gold was recovered. After the 1960s not much placer mining was done on Wild Horse Creek—but this creek remains an excellent creek to pan and prospect as it has never released all of its gold.

Bull River ★★

The Bull River was found to contain placer gold in 1882 below the long canyon, and it was felt at that time that the gold came from veins in the canyon area. Crevasses in the bedrock of the river were producing gold in good quantities in 1883. In 1884, the Bull River produced some $17,232 worth of gold by hand methods with gold valued at approximately $13 per ounce. This was an impressive accomplishment considering that no roads existed at the time. In 1885 $5,100 worth of gold was recovered notwithstanding the fact that new creeks and diggings were being discovered and mini gold rushes to other creeks were the order of day.

Bull River is a good-sized stream, swift and broad, until it enters the canyon, where it is confined to a width of about 9 metres (30 feet). Through this gorge, approximately 1 kilometre long, the river drops some 90 metres (300 feet) in a succession of falls and rapids. Here it rushes along, lashed into foam, as two sharp right-angled turns obstruct its passage. It straightens out in a mad dash forward and then drops out of sight over falls some 24 metres (80 feet) high, which reflect a rainbow in the sunlight. Below this, the river plunges about half a kilometre. Suddenly the canyon widens into a valley with sloping sides through which the river peacefully winds. The canyon of the Bull River forms some of the most spectacular scenery in the area.

Continued high water in 1887 saw no steady work done on the Bull River even though some very rich deposits were found. The gold was coarse and easily recovered. The paying gravels were found on both sides of the river along its length below the long canyon. By 1895 people were tunnelling to reach an old channel of the river. By 1898 it was reported that the gold was recovered from the river for about a kilometre above and below the canyon. The gold recovered here was very coarse and very clean with very few other minerals present.

The source of gold in the Bull River has been speculated upon but never found. Gold remains in the river above and below the canyon area today. It is an excellent area to prospect and pan or just visit because of its spectacular views.

Quartz Creek ✶✶

Flowing into the Columbia River at Beavermouth on the CPR rail line, Quartz Creek has long been known as a good placer creek. The old workings are hardly visible today and most of the old cabins have fallen down and rotted away. Gold was known to exist and was found some 150 metres (500 feet) above the creek. The presence of an old channel is likely in this creek area. Leases were attached in the area, which is approximately

CPR wooden bridge over Quartz Creek, 1900. VANCOUVER PUBLIC LIBRARY 858

1,800 metres (6,000 feet) above sea level. The distance up the creek is between 16 and 37 kilometres (10 and 23 miles).

Prospecting of this creek was carried on in 1935 with good results obtained by hand work. Not much mining was ever done on this creek, and it remains an excellent creek to prospect and pan for gold.

A very small pit was excavated on Quartz Creek in 1926, and 369 grams (13 ounces) of rough, coarse gold was found. Due to the lateness of the season, no more was done. All the supplies had to be packed in by hand over what was a rough track at the time.

Forty-Nine Creek ✶✶✶

Located near Nelson, Forty-Nine Creek has long been known as a placer creek. By 1880 about nine miners were working on the creek and doing well. A trial clean-up from 55 metres (60 yards) of gravel in 1894 recovered over a kilogram (42 ounces) of gold, an astonishing amount for the volume of gravel. The miners were amazed at their good fortune but a lack of water shut down the operation that year. These workings were located on the creek some 14 kilometres (nine miles) west of Nelson. Every small portion of the area was worked and yielded over $4,000 in gold at the prices then set. This would be approximately 9.5 kilograms (335 ounces) of gold.

After the turn of the century many miners were searching for— and finding—the vein where the gold originated, and placer mining did not take place on any large scale. By 1914 interest was renewed on Forty-Nine Creek and heavy coarse gold was again being recovered. Less than 16 kilometres (10 miles) from Nelson, the creek could be accessed by one of the few good roads of the day. Five creek leases (each lease 75 metres, or 250 feet, in length) were taken out, and testing and prospecting was done. By 1915 a tunnel was being driven

Looking up the Kootenay River, from Naksup and Slocan Railway, Nelson, BC, circa 1905. CITY OF VANCOUVER ARCHIVES, AM54-S4-: OUT P716.2

to intercept the old channel here. Coarse gold was recovered that year and good progress was made. By 1916 plans were being made to wash the old channel area, and miners were so confident that a house was constructed on the property. This hydraulic plant would have a washing capacity of 183 metres (200 yards) per day. By 1921 two men were working on the creek recovering gold. In 1933 work was done on the bench area on the northeastern side of the creek at a point approximately one kilometre above the road leading to Nelson's power plant on the Kootenay River. Gold was being recovered in good quantities in the area. Not much placer mining was carried on after the Second World War, and this creek remains an excellent creek to prospect and pan.

Hall Creek ✶✶

In 1891 Hall Creek was producing good results. The area worked was some 19 kilometres (12 miles) south of Nelson, and in 1892 good prospects were being found yielding considerable gold to the miners. In 1893 one lease was being worked with good results. One lease on Hall Creek yielded some $1,250 worth of gold, or nearly 3 kilograms (105 ounces), to two miners working by hand during a very short season. By 1895 the yield of gold was as great but less work was done than the previous year. By 1904 a small company had been formed to work these placer leases at the mouth of Hall Creek on the banks as well as the streambed itself. Testing was being done before any type of mining commenced.

By the 1930s, Hall Creek was still producing gold in good quantities, with over 28 kilograms (1,000 ounces) being recovered in a single year by individuals working alone and in very small groups. In 1935 31 kilograms (1,101 ounces) were recovered. Hall Creek remains today an excellent area for placer panning.

INDEX OF CREEKS

ABOUT THE AUTHORS

Born in New Brunswick, *Jim Lewis* moved west in the early 1960s to prospect for gold. He has been staking claims all over BC and Yukon ever since. He has owned and operated several BC placer mines and worked as a consultant for both placer and hardrock mining. He lives in Clearwater, British Columbia.

Born in a small farming village in Essex, England, *Susan Campany* worked for a large mining company in London as secretary to the chief mining engineer and geologist before she immigrated to Canada in 1972. She met and married Jim Lewis in 1998 and enjoyed the practical side of gold panning for many years. She once commented, "If a person from the heart of the English countryside can learn to gold pan and enjoy it, anyone can!" Susan died in 2013.